Hot tips on witnessing:

- Be creative
- Just keep loving people — their curiosity will compel them to ask "why?"
- Avoid "churchy" language and cliches like "Jesus is the answer to..." and "Are you in the Word?"
- Keep in mind that it's human nature for people to not want to be saved from their sins

These are but a few of the many pointers you'll receive from ***The Art of Sharing Your Faith.*** This book will assure you that witnessing can be a rewarding adventure in faith.

THE ART OF SHARING YOUR FAITH

JOEL D. HECK, EDITOR

Fleming H. Revell Company
Tarrytown, New York

Library of Congress Cataloging-in-Publication Data

The art of sharing your faith / Joel D. Heck, editor.
p. cm.
Includes bibliographical references.
ISBN 0-8007-5387-9
1. Witness bearing (Christianity) I. Heck, Joel D.
BV4520.A78 1991 90-48506
248'.5—dc20 CIP

Published by the Fleming H. Revell Company
Tarrytown, New York 10591
Printed in the United States of America

TO my father, Donald E. Heck,
whose concern for mission
was one of the key motivations for this book

Contents

Foreword

Years ago, the late Jonathan Dolliver gave a dinner for a number of dignitaries in Washington, D. C. In the gathering were congressional leaders, cabinet members, judges, and a sprinkling of foreign diplomats. Also present was Senator Dolliver's father, a retired Methodist preacher.

After dinner, while the guests lingered to visit, the senator noticed his father conversing with one of the prominent ambassadors. As he approached them, Senator Dolliver overheard his father gently say, "My brother, how is it with your soul?" Thinking that the question was a bit out of place, he edged his way between them, and the father retired. Soon the diplomat also went his way.

Some time afterward, the Reverend Dolliver died. At the funeral there were many beautiful floral tributes. But one stood out above all the rest. The flowers were rare and exquisitely arranged. Attached to them was a small card, and on it, over the signature of a distinguished ambassador, were written these words: "To the man who cared for my soul."

The old preacher's message had not been forgotten, nor the love of Jesus that constrained him to care. He had learned the art of witnessing.

This is a skill and a life-style every disciple of Christ should cultivate. The way in which we share the Gospel, of course, will differ from person to person. God has endowed all of us with unique temperaments and gifts that will be reflected in the manner of our witness. But however variable the presentation, as well as the situations in which we live, we must seek to point lost men and women to the Savior. Apart from prayer, no Christian discipline has more eternal significance.

That is why this book is so pertinent. It comes to grips with the issues of the soul and in down-to-earth, practical guidelines helps us know how to communicate more effectively the good news of salvation.

Each chapter addresses a vital area of concern, and, taken together, they cover a wide range of interests. The variety of authors adds depth and perspective to the collection. Rarely, if ever, has a more representative panel of authorities on the subject been assembled in one volume.

What makes the treatment believable is the realism of the instructors. No armchair counselors, they write as practitioners, not theoreticians. The advice offered here has been forged on the anvil of experience over many years of active ministry.

Teachers with these credentials have earned the right to be heard, and it is with genuine anticipation that I invite you to join me in sitting at their feet. This may well be one of the most rewarding books you will ever read on personal evangelism.

ROBERT E. COLEMAN

Introduction

Welcome to a study of life-style evangelism. In the chapters that follow, you will study basic skills for sharing your faith in Jesus Christ. Many of these skills you already know; others will be quite new to you. But whether you are studying this book on your own or working through the book with a group, you will become a more effective Christian witness to the extent that you understand and apply the insights of these writers.

When we call this *The Art of Sharing Your Faith,* we are not talking about art in the sense of Michelangelo or Leonardo da Vinci. We are talking about art in the sense of a skill or an ability. Sharing your faith is a skill that can be learned. While the Holy Spirit is the best teacher, the people who wrote these chapters can also help you communicate your faith.

The authors of these chapters come from different states, different organizations, and different denominations. Consequently, they will express how people come to faith in various ways.

Read a chapter a week. The chapters are arranged sequentially, beginning with who you are in Christ (chapter 1), your spiritual growth in Christ (chapter 2), building a relationship (chapters 3, 4), learning communication skills (chapters 5–9), and dealing with specific types of people (chapters 10–13).

If you are working with a group, discuss the questions at the end of each chapter. The thirteen chapters fit nicely into one quarter of a year's curriculum. If you are working alone, think through the questions on your own. Then take a week to look for ways to apply what you have learned. Use the world around you as your laboratory; the authors of these chapters have used that same lab to discover the principles they share with you in each chapter.

Many of the insights from chapters 1–9 apply to the specific situations addressed in chapters 10–13. We have not asked the authors of the final four chapters to reinvent the wheel but rather to assume that basic principles for witnessing have appeared in the first nine chapters.

Furthermore, please note the motivation for all Christian witnessing, whether an author mentions it explicitly or implies it. Christians witness because God has so blessed them with the gift of faith that they want others to have that same faith in Jesus Christ. In other words, the message of the Gospel motivates you to tell others. "We love because he first loved us" (1 John 4:19). Part of that love expresses itself in witnessing, so we also witness because He first loved us. Only a Spirit-filled believer can respond in obedience to Christ's commands to "make disciples of all nations" (Matthew 28:19), to "proclaim . . . the eternal life" (1 John 1:2), "to give an answer to everyone who asks you to give the reason for the hope that you have" (1 Peter 3:15).

THE ART OF SHARING YOUR FAITH

1
the art of being human

ann kiemel anderson

i was fresh out of college. a bachelor of arts degree under my arm. more confident than i had ever been or would be again. en route to kansas city, missouri, to teach junior high history and english. my school was located on the kansas side of the line, and i taught upper-middle-class students.

the senior minister at the large church i attended preached every sunday about saving the world. reaching the lost. giving sight to the blind.

i was overwhelmed.

how did we *really* do that?

at a very secular school?

in the late sixties when separation of church and state was a major issue?

a passion for "lost" people began to burn in me. i was

twenty-one years old, young and naive and inexperienced. but my heart was pure. i was desperately hungry for more of God and consumed with a search to lead others to him.

every night i would walk into the house where i rented a room. before taking off my coat or dropping the stack of books and papers in my arms, i would fall on my knees just inside the door.

"oh, Jesus," i sobbed, "please show me how to really do this. please help me to lead some of my students to you."

my father was my spiritual mentor, and he and my mother brought the world into our home. servicemen ate at our table. my grandfather had read the Bible one hundred times on his knees by the bed, and on every visit, my father would show me the worn spots in the wood where he knelt.

yet our lives were so deeply entwined in the church that somehow i had grown up inviting people to church, but not to Jesus.

one afternoon, between classes, i boldly walked out into the hall. shaking with fear, i started reaching out to students.

grabbing one boy's arm, i asked,

"do you go to church anywhere?"

"uh, no, miss kiemel. . . ."

"would you go to church with me? i will buy you a mcdonald's hamburger and coke afterward. . . ."

hamburgers were then fifteen cents apiece. imagine! it was the one ploy i could think of.

the first sunday, i had three students go to church with me. probably because they were afraid not to. i was a teacher who asked, and they were taught to please teachers.

a week rolled by, and i had five students the next sunday. my little karman ghia was stuffed. how was i going to continue this dream?

after that morning service, i walked up the aisle to the senior minister.

"you preach about saving the world. i do not know very much about it, but i have brought students from my school the last two sundays. i was wondering if . . . well . . . would you let me use one of the church buses next week? i think i can fill it."

"well, ann, your school is across town. that seems a little extreme. but . . . let's try it for one or two sundays."

i was ecstatic and began feverishly working to pack that bus with kids. that sunday, and many sundays after, i began filling the bus with junior high squeals and laughter and spirit.

every sunday, i would walk down the aisle of the large sanctuary with two or three dozen kids behind me. inevitably some little woman would tap me and say,

"does the principal know this?"

i would shudder in horror at the very thought. the secular principal was an awesome figure in my life and one i was terrified of.

one morning, i decided i must go in and tell the principal because integrity demanded it. i was sure it would be the last day of my teaching career, but so be it.

"mr. wallace, i just thought you should know that i have been filling a bus every sunday with students from our school. it seems to me that kids need more than head knowledge to make it in this world, and i have been sharing Jesus."

i said it all in one big sentence, looking him straight in the eye. not flinching. already, i had led two or three of the students to a personal faith in Jesus. i was learning how to really share the Lord, and nothing could have stopped me.

mr. wallace leaned back in his big chair (it seemed massive to me) and smiled.

"ann, i know you have been doing this. . . ."

i sat very still. hardly breathing. total eye contact. he already knew?

"the parents have been calling. telling me about it. they are very pleased. they cannot imagine a teacher caring enough to spend a sixth day with their children. as long as they are happy, you can continue."

my father WAS right. he really did understand. following Jesus DID pay. i floated out of mr. wallace's office.

nothing ever deterred me again. that was the genesis of my sharing Jesus so freely. it was the most commanding adventure i had ever experienced. i was ordinary. human. simple. unknown. yet i, ann, could tell ANYONE about the Living Lord!

so many who grow up in Christian homes have no passion. Jesus is another word. a casual experience. my parents felt passion about Jesus, and their mantle fell on me. maybe we are too in love with a church and not God himself.

from kansas city, i received a call to be the youth director of a large nazarene church in long beach, california.

there were eighty-eight kids in the junior high and senior high departments combined. one of the most defiant boys in the group was a high schooler whose father was on the board. several warned me that i dare not touch him.

my first sunday morning, i was shocked to discover kids throwing spit-wads across the spacious youth room. standing on chairs. yelling. it was intolerable to me. i had been a teacher who did not smile the first two weeks to command some control and authority. now i was in God's house, and these kids were far worse than any i had encountered in the public school. i noticed the board member's son was one of the spit-wad throwers.

"hi, i am ann. your new youth director. i do not demand

that you follow Jesus, for that is personal. i cannot demand that you be deeply committed, for that is personal, too. BUT i CAN insist that you will not be a part of this youth group unless you have the decency to respect God. if you do not, i will see that you leave the room while we worship!"

i was a teacher, and i laid down the law accordingly. i challenged them to prove me, and they did!

that night, my first sunday, in the large sanctuary, all the youth sat cloistered in the left, front section. jimmy, the board member's son, was three rows behind me, and he would not stop cutting up with his friends.

as the senior minister rose to present the evening message, i stood . . . walked three rows back . . . and motioned for jimmy to leave. the minister stalled, and one thousand pair of eyes quietly watched.

i did not move until jimmy walked down the aisle to the back pew, and the usher seated him there. then i sat down, and the minister proceeded.

my face felt blazing red. my eyes filled with tears. my heart was pounding. why had i ever made such a threat? one i had to be true to?

in my heart, i wanted these teenagers to change the world. how can you love Jesus enough to share Him if you do not even respect Him?

after the service, i did not run to jimmy and say,

"i am sorry. i made a threat, and i had to follow through on it."

i wrote him a note saying i loved him. that i would do it again if i had to. that i saw such potential in him, and i was determined to help God unearth it.

i crawled in my little car, and blindly drove from one southern california freeway to another until i found jimmy's house. it was very late, and when he answered the door, i simply smiled. handed him the note . . . and drove away.

after that first night, i initiated a relationship with him. he loved to surf, and i would go early mornings, before school, and watch him. cheer him. afternoons, i would bring him a coke, and sit on his front step, and let him tell me his girl problems. i really loved him, but he knew i would dismiss him from church if he lost his respect for the Lord.

jimmy became one of my finest, purest, most dedicated teenagers. i had called him to something greater than himself, and no one ever had before.

every day then (and now), i would pray, "Jesus, make me creative. give me ideas for my world."

in every corner, i watched for opportunities. wherever there was a need, i tried to meet it.

one afternoon, a chunky junior high boy came into my office at the church.

"could my buddy and i use your parking lot to play football? the lady out there told me to ask you."

obviously, one of the church secretaries had sent him down the hall to me.

"sure, you can, IF you and your friend will first let me spend thirty minutes with you, talking about God."

he thought a minute.

"okay," he grinned.

that was the beginning of my junior high boys' club. every week this kid brought more and more of his friends to my office. we developed a wonderful relationship. for thirty minutes we talked about their struggles and dreams, and i shared some Scripture and God's love.

one morning, the mother of this adolescent called. not a spiritual person at all.

"ann, this is scott's mother. i have never seen scott so excited about anything as he is about meeting with you every week. i was wondering if maybe i could provide refreshments for the boys on wednesdays?"

it was a perfect idea. now i had the chance to reach out to scott's mother and father. to tell them about the Lord.

never did i try to entertain my teenagers. i called them to a mission. i tried to give them a vision to live and die for. a dream.

"if you really want to help change the world," i would often say, "then meet me at the church altar saturday morning at 5:30 a.m." one had to sacrifice. to pay a price. to run to win. teenagers, more than anyone i know, can be challenged to scale the mountaintop if someone will just lead them there.

i do not believe i ever asked my teens to do anything that i first did not do myself. to teach them how to love each other, i, personally, individually, loved them.

every morning, i would call a few of them before they raced out the front door for school.

"marlene, what time is your date tonight?"

"7:00 p.m."

"are you excited?"

"oh, ann . . . yesss . . . !

"i love you, marlene. i am excited, too. and i am praying for you."

many of the teens started wanting me to teach a Bible study in their homes. they had to find two friends to join them, and then i would come. i drove all over southern california freeways to teens' homes and watched incredible growth as new kids brought *their* friends the next week.

one morning a month, i solicited some parent to help me. we fixed pancakes and bacon and orange juice in the fellowship hall for high schoolers. 5:30 in the morning . . . before school. a couple hundred kids would pour in the doors from the black, early-morning darkness. we charged a quarter from each one, and after breakfast sang together, and i led them in a devotional before they headed out to the war zone of peers and school pressure.

we grew from eighty-eight rowdy, disrespectful teenagers to sometimes 300–400 deeply committed, reverent, very excited dreamers.

we asked God for the impossible. we sacrificed. we learned to love each other, and then God gave us the world. i tried to make them tough in their faith. i tried not to cut any corners.

if john's grandmother was sick, i went to see her because she was so important to john. always trying to find a need to meet, and out of that came new blessings in sharing Jesus.

i prayed with major high school football teams before their games and saw the miracle of pat boone coming to our church, even though no one believed he would (except the teens and me).

rather than telling my teenagers to bring their Bibles, i simply always carried mine and read from it to them. again, trying to guide them by example.

when i left california to go to boston, to be dean of women on a college campus, i wept. i knew i must never hold to anything too tightly . . . except God . . . yet i was leaving several hundred teenagers who had found the latch that opens the door to God. no adventure in the world can be more exciting than that.

in boston, i was in a totally different arena. there, i was in charge of hundreds of college girls and dormitory assistants and faculty advisors. i had discipline issues to resolve. conflicts between girls.

i baked dozens of chocolate chip cookies. drove to a dormitory. called all the girls on one floor together. we chewed on the cookies and talked about struggles.

one girl was very bright but so plain. i quietly slipped her a new dress and told her to keep this a secret. several months later, she bumped into me as i was flying through the student union building to a meeting.

"martha, you look beautiful! i LOVE your dress! where did you get that?" i had forgotten my gift of previous months, so she looked at me curiously.

"ann, you bought me this dress."

i laughed. hugged her. felt terribly embarrassed.

evangelism touches everybody. it becomes a way of life. it is a spontaneous response in all situations. it became a part of the way i breathed and felt and lived.

never did i drive into a gas station and say to myself,

"i had better witness to this attendant. i am a Christian, so i must do that."

and then find my hands sweaty. my heart pounding. nervous and afraid. i started outside the junior high classroom. but i was no longer there. now, talking about Jesus was as natural as licking an ice-cream cone.

often . . . daily . . . i shared my love for Jesus with taxicab drivers, with airline pilots, with construction workers, and neighbors. businessmen and young mothers, and most of all, children in less-fortunate neighborhoods.

one day, i boarded a flight for a speaking engagement. an impeccably dressed, strong-looking man sat next to me.

"do you live in chicago?"

"no, i am just going there to speak," i replied, smiling.

"what do you speak about?"

"do you *really* want to know?"

"yes. . . ."

"about Jesus, and His love, and that He and I can change the world."

he appeared astonished.

"well . . . that is very interesting. i have a beautiful wife, five great kids, a terrific job, and i do not have anything to do with God. what do you think about that?"

"sir, you CAN have a great family and a good life

without God . . . at least for a time. . . . but you can never have the BEST, for only God knows what that is. sir, i am an ordinary young woman, but i am not willing to settle for anything but the BEST."

his eyes instantly filled with tears.

"that is a very unique concept," he replied.

for the entire flight we shared an animated conversation about following Jesus. it was one of thousands of conversations i have had with people about Jesus.

when you pray for Jesus to make you creative, you are amazed at how utterly creative the Author of Creation can be!

i have taken ghetto children on speaking trips with me. had waitresses come to my apartment after work and find Jesus over cookies and hot chocolate. built a gymnasium in the basement of a sturdy, old ghetto building for all the strong, young children to play in. the alleys and crowded streets had been their arena before.

it became very natural for me to sing little songs to people. i did not do it to be like anyone, or because i had a good voice, but only because it just happened one day while sharing with a neighbor. she loved the little song so much that i tried it again with someone else. always, it amazed me to see the tears and warm, unexpected responses.

sometimes, people would develop a rather strange look on their faces when i suggested singing a song. sometimes they asked me to keep it down to a soft tone. BUT, without exception, they all seemed to catch the pure, earnest spontaneity of my heart and were rather captured and touched.

in evangelism, you do not share Jesus the way everyone else does. each person has a unique personality, and God will fashion a plan for you built around your very own strengths and abilities.

you never take on a superior position, either. along with being truly genuine is the importance of equality. i do not believe i have ever felt i was good and the other person was bad. or that i was righteous and he/she was a sinner. i simply try to touch people at their point of need, for that is where everyone comes to Jesus in true surrender. and i never ever forget i am a sinner saved by GRACE, and i will always have feet of clay, too.

one morning, in boston, i awakened and thought,

"i could become a runner. then i could run beside all the other runners, and sing them little songs, and say prayers for them."

well, i had always been a dreamer. i was thirty-four years old and knew no dream lived easily. BUT i actually thought this might not be too hard because i had never been an athlete, and watching people sort of glide by looked easy! oh, such innocence . . . and ignorance!

i discovered, quickly, that i hated running. that it was not easy. that, in fact, it was the hardest thing i had ever done. but i was determined, and nothing deterred me.

with eight 26.2 mile marathons under my belt (two in israel, two in boston, etc.), i now have had the beautiful opportunity of singing and praying with hundreds of runners.

in the early morning, i would head out for the charles river and pick a runner up ahead of me. i would run as fast as i could (great speed workout) to catch up with that runner so i could share with him or her while we ran. usually we were both miserable enough to love the distraction!

today, i am married with four very small (ages five, four, two and one) sons. before we redid the big family place in the country and moved out there, we lived in a typical neighborhood.

every day, i would pray for the family that built the big,

white house behind us. they kept the most perfectly manicured yard in the neighborhood. their children were wonderful and baby-sat for me since taylor, my first, was a baby. linda, the wife and mother, is younger than i but a peer.

one day, she knocked at my door. i was home, alone, because i had become terribly ill and had to cancel a women's convention in the south. someone had taken my children for the day, and will was on a business trip.

God is so perfect in His timing. with His plans. He is far more concerned about individuals than He is with large groups. He grounded me from speaking to hundreds so i would be home when my neighbor knocked. and He used a kitty to create the encounter.

"ann, we have lost our kitten. we all love her so much, and bob has been in every backyard in the neighborhood . . . every empty lot. we cannot find her anywhere. could i come through and check your backyard?"

linda stood on my porch, fresh and beautiful . . . yet troubled. i had a high fever. could hardly stand up. hated for *anyone* to see me in such awful shape.

"well, yes, linda . . . of course. come on through, and go out back. i have not seen any kitties, but . . ."

my mother never liked cats. we always had dogs. i did not understand the emotion and bonding to that little kitty. i only knew she was my neighbor. i loved her, and i had prayed for her for six and a half years.

linda came in from our deck, defeated. no kitty in sight.

instantly, standing there, i said,

"linda, why don't we pray for your kitten? God knows everything. He knows exactly where she is."

linda kind of laughed.

"pray for a kitty? that seems kind of silly. . . ."

"i do not think so," i responded. "i pray about everything. please."

i took linda's hand and began praying.

"Jesus, you know exactly where that cat is. You love bob and linda. You care about what they feel. please hear this simple prayer and bring the kitty back."

i hugged linda, and she headed for the door, where she stopped. she started talking about other things, and i grew weak and sat down on the little end table by one of the sofas. suddenly, as if in an audible voice, God seemed to say,

"ann, i kept you home from that convention for linda!"

suddenly, looking into linda's face, i said, "linda, you are not ready to go home yet, are you?"

"no," she responded, instantly crying. "oh, no. ann, my life is so stressed out, and i do not know how i am going to make it."

"linda, have i ever specifically told you how to personally accept Jesus into your life? let me get a piece of paper. . . ."

for most of us, it is very easy to reach out to someone who is really hurting. often, however, we generalize God. . . . tell them we will pray for them. . . . but we never get down to the simple, pure issue. . . . do you know Jesus personally? well, can i tell you how you can?

with linda, i cut across all the issues to that truth. i knew (from the Holy Spirit guiding me that very moment) that i needed to give her the Cure . . . and not just relieve her pain by letting her talk and cry.

i always use several points from bill bright's "four spiritual laws." the circles of trusting and trying. revelation 3:20 about Jesus standing at our heart's door.

"oh, ann, how do i know this is truth?" linda sobbed,

"what about the temple, and all the ceremonies we have been through as a family?"

they were on the outside perimeters of a large, institutionalized religion.

"linda, only Jesus is truth. but i will not try to talk you into this. it is a very personal decision that only you can make. for me . . . well, it has changed my entire life."

"ann, i cannot leave your house without God . . . and you are the only one i know who really knows Him. . . ."

linda continued to sob.

"linda, do you see Jesus in this room?"

"yes. . . ." she immediately spoke.

"where?"

"right here, sitting next to me."

"can you see His face?"

"yes . . . it is full of love and kindness."

i was in awe. i had never asked anyone those questions before. again the Holy Spirit was making me creative. and it all seemed to clarify the loose pieces in her mind.

in one of the most dramatic, beautiful conversions i have ever witnessed, linda confessed her sins and genuinely invited Jesus into her life. her face was absolutely shining. as she walked out my front door, i called out,

"linda, you will find your kitty. i just know you will."

she turned around and said,

"ann, how am i going to tell my family about this? they will not understand."

"linda, God will show you. today, unless He shows you otherwise, just bask in His love. He will lead you through the other areas."

often, when people come to Jesus, it is a process. conversion, and then the Holy Spirit showing them how to clean up their lives. if the conversion is genuine, they will begin to change. but they will not be perfected overnight.

about four hours later, i called linda. i assumed the devil would probably be trying to talk her out of this courageous, outlandish decision.

"how are you, linda?"

"oh, i have more peace than i ever have had, but i keep thinking about my family. they will think i have gone nuts."

we talked awhile. i listened a lot. reassured her.

"have you found the kitten yet?"

"oh, no, ann. . . . she is lost forever, i fear."

just as i hung the telephone receiver back on the wall, i heard "meow . . . meow . . ." and scraping on the screen door off the deck. i grabbed the levolor string, pulled up the blind, and there was a little black kitty with a white nose and white paws.

hurriedly, i dialed linda's number.

"is your kitty black? with white paws and a white nose?"

"yes . . . yes. . . ."

"well, she is meowing on my back deck. . . ."

linda screamed. i heard bob yell. a few minutes later he was limping onto my deck, for he had somehow scaled the high wall that divided our yards. with tears in his eyes, he grabbed the kitty and said he would call me as soon as he got home.

"ann, linda told me about your day. this is such a miracle. it makes me want to believe!"

can you beat that? can anything be more fun than following Jesus? is it not amazing that in a world teeming with billions of people, He cares about the lindas of the world? about me? about you?

it is with humble pride that i share my faith in Jesus. i am NOT ashamed of the gospel of Jesus Christ. every day is a new adventure. a fresh surprise.

i do not care to push my children to earn ph.d.s or make millions of dollars. to be a star on the basketball team or be applauded by thousands. oh, no, i only long for them to totally embrace Jesus and to share His power and His love with a lost, desperate, very hurting world.

every day i pray,
"Jesus, humiliate me if You must, but keep me pure. . . . and help will and me to inspire our children to honor You."
will you join me in this dream?

Discussion Questions

1. In what ways do Christians cease to be themselves as they begin to witness? How was ann kiemel refreshingly herself? With jimmy and with linda?

2. What gets in the way of being ourselves?

3. What are some of the advantages of being yourself, open and transparent? Why would this help you to be a better witness?

4. What are some of the potential pitfalls?

5. Respond to these words: "evangelism touches everybody. it becomes a way of life. it is a spontaneous response in all situations. it became a part of the way i breathed and felt and lived."

6. Why must we treat other people with equality?

7. In what ways was Jesus open with people? In what ways did He treat them with respect? *See*, for example, Luke 19:5 and John 8:3–11.

8. How is Jesus really the key to ann's witness, both as to the content of her witness and the style of her witness? How can He be the same for you?

2
The Art of Growing in Christ

Mark McCloskey

A few years ago, a friend asked me a profound question: "What puts a smile on your face and a fire in your heart?" Since then, I have asked myself this question every week or so. I like it because it's one of those "life questions" that probes to the core of our spiritual and motivational being.

On a surface level, my answer varies from day to day (nothing today, baseball or pasta tomorrow). If I go to a deeper motivational level, my answer is usually the same (my family, friends, and ministry opportunities). But the answer I and every believer find at the core of our being, our heart of hearts, is always and only Jesus. Just Jesus—growing in our knowledge of Him and making Him known.

These deep concerns of the heart are the focus of this chapter. We'll discuss how our growth in knowing Him relates to our growth in making Him known. We'll look at how evangelism results from and contributes to the personal transformation God has initiated by His grace in each of our lives.

Growth: Our Winsome Walk Toward Wholeness

Probably none of us is content with our present level of development in character and conduct. Each honest heart must admit that we are not yet what we were created to be or want to be. We want to change, move ahead, and take new ground. Most of all, we want to know Jesus more deeply.

These desires are evidence of the God-given drive in every Christian's heart for spiritual growth. For most of us, a considerable part of our waking moments is spent seeking wholeness in the face of our incompleteness. Each of us craves integration and healing for our divided and broken selves. Each of us, reflecting our design in God's image, seeks out opportunities to close the distance between who we are and the person we know God wants us to become.

Given our need to grow, it is a joyful truth that Jesus' call to follow Him is the call to join Him in a winsome walk toward wholeness. It is the call to cooperate with Him as He reclaims for us all that we have lost to the Fall. It is the call to "grow in the grace and knowledge of our Lord and Savior Jesus Christ" (2 Peter 3:18).

Only God Causes Growth

But here we must pause to highlight an irony of the Christian life. Authentic growth comes not from seeking growth as an end in itself but from being caught up in the purposes and plans of the One who causes the growth. "I planted the seed, Apollos watered it, but God made it grow" (1 Corinthians 3:6). We experience authentic growth only as Jesus walks daily with us. Jesus walks daily with us as He speaks to us in His word.

As we grow in our walk with Him, God will clear our path to save us from the disappointment and certain failure which plague our self-help generation. For the road to growth outside of God's plan is filled with dead ends and false gods, offering less-than-satisfying substitutes for our pursuit of wholeness and well-being. Sadly, those who give their lives in search of personal growth, while ignoring the Source of growth, may experience many things along the way, but never the personal transformation that comes from knowing Jesus.

So, while the Scriptures tell us to "grow in the grace and knowledge of our Lord and Savior Jesus Christ" (2 Peter 3:18), we are reminded that even as we are commanded to grow, it is God and God alone who causes the growth.

A Joyful Effort

How does spiritual growth come about in our lives? Is it effortless and natural, or is it a matter of discipline and hard work? Is it joyful or difficult? Of course, the answer is "all of the above." It would be a mistake to assume that just because something is natural, it must also be easy; or just because something is difficult, it must therefore be unnatural.

Growth results as God works in our lives through a variety of means and circumstances: the Word, the testimonies of Christian people, worship, and more. At times our growth is difficult, requiring strenuous effort. At times our growth comes almost without effort, the result of spontaneous inner change. But however God chooses to work in our lives, whether through difficulty or with relative ease, the same Holy Spirit controls the growth process.

Pictures of Growth

The Scriptures use many images to describe the growth process. Christian growth is pictured as a building in the process of construction, plants growing to maturity, and darkness giving way to light. But the image of exchanging dirty clothes for clean especially helps to show how God produces growth in our lives.

This "clothing exchange" could be called the "displacement" view of growth. As Paul writes, "Rather, clothe yourselves with the Lord Jesus Christ, and do not think about how to gratify the desires of the sinful nature" (Romans 13:14) and "Do not lie to each other, since you have taken off your old self with its practices and have put on the new self, which is being renewed in knowledge in the image of its Creator" (Colossians 3:9, 10).

The great nineteenth-century Scottish preacher Thomas Chalmers spelled out this approach to growth in his classic sermon, "The Expulsive Power of a New Affection." As Chalmers saw it, the Scriptures teach that growth comes not from force without (conformity to rules and regulations or revulsion with the vanity of the world) but from power within (through the attractive, transforming work of Jesus in our inner self).

Spiritual growth can be understood as the exchange of an old affection for the new, the love of the world for the love of Jesus. In Chalmers' words, "We require an affection that, when seated on the throne of our life, either subordinates or purifies every other affection or else casts it out."[1]

As we "clothe ourselves with Jesus Christ" (*see* Romans 13:14) and allow Him to assume His rightful role as King of our lives, He becomes that "master affection" that will "cast out" or displace the habits and deep-seated motivations that plague our lives and stunt our growth. This displacement is a process of inner transformation made possible by the presence and power of the Holy Spirit working through the Word (Romans 12:2).

This growth process is not to be confused with behavior modification. God is never content only to change us on the outside just to get us to do the right thing. He wants nothing less than our inward transformation. God wants us to do the right things for the right reasons from a glad heart. "We love because he first loved us" (1 John 4:19). Even animals (e.g., Pavlov's dogs) can be made to change their behavior by exposing them to the correct combination of external stimuli. But only God can change the human heart.

Preoccupation With Jesus

Spiritual growth results as we keep our focus on our affection. Yes, it is entirely true that we must concern ourselves with avoiding the negative. Paul warned Timothy to "flee the evil desires of youth" (2 Timothy 2:22). He warned the Romans to "put to death the misdeeds of the body" (Romans 8:13). But the overall emphasis of the Scriptures is not on what to avoid but rather on who and what to pursue. We are to "fix our eyes on Jesus" (Hebrews 12:2) and "pursue righteousness, faith, love and peace" (2 Timothy 2:22).

We move ahead in the Christian life not because the alternative options are so dreadful and dangerous (and they are) but because Jesus Christ, our new affection, is so attractive. Growth is the compelling, joyful pursuit of

Jesus. In this sense, our growth is not so much a matter of giving up negative things as it is losing interest in them. We grow as we become so preoccupied with Jesus that we simply do not have the time, interest, or place in our lives for the pursuit of sin. Our new affection for Him leaves room for nothing else. As Chalmers wrote, "There is no better way to keep the love of the world out of our hearts than to keep in our hearts the love of God."

Now that we have laid the foundation for an understanding of spiritual growth, we can explore how our growth relates to the practice of personal evangelism. There is an essential, mutually beneficial relationship between evangelism and spiritual growth that is often overlooked.

Evangelism Results From Growing in Him

In New Testament times, involvement in personal evangelism wasn't so much the pinnacle of a lengthy growth process as it was an initial response to the joy of conversion and the goodness of God (*read* especially Acts 2—8). In fact, I believe that evangelism is one of our first steps of spiritual growth.

The Overflow of a Glad Heart

Think for a moment. How did Jesus get His followers to tell others about Him? The formula, if we could use such a word, was simply this: Jesus changed their lives. He saved them. He loved them. The result: followers of Jesus so transformed and so grateful that sharing the Good News of their wonderful Savior was the first thing on their minds.

The woman at the well (John 4:39–42) was so impressed with Jesus that she immediately told her whole town about Him, with the result that many believed when they came to see Jesus for themselves.

Andrew couldn't wait to tell Peter that he had found the Messiah (John 1:41, 42), and after meeting Jesus, Philip wasted no time in asking Nathanael to "come and see" Jesus for himself (John 1:43–51).

Soon after quitting his tax-gathering to follow Jesus, Matthew, out of a heart of gratitude, threw a big party at his home for Jesus and invited his tax-gatherer and "sinner" friends to meet Him (Matthew 9:9–12).

The Gerasene demoniac departed from Jesus a changed man and immediately returned to his home territory to tell others "how much Jesus had done for him" (Mark 5:1–20).

These stories leave us with the vivid impression that evangelism is simply a matter of grateful people telling others about their dearest Friend. Or as D. T. Niles put it, "Evangelism is one beggar telling another beggar where they may both find bread."[2] The pattern is quite clear. When Jesus changes us through the Gospel, we can't help but share with others the Good News of His surprising grace.

But how does this work in our lives?

The Holy Spirit Produces Our Growth

No discussion of either spiritual growth or evangelism would be possible or profitable without focusing our attention on the ministry of the Holy Spirit, for He is the crucial factor in coming to a biblical understanding of both.

The gift of the Holy Spirit at Pentecost gave the church an incurable case of spiritual claustrophobia. Involvement in evangelism became a natural expression of the early church's life. By the very nature of their identity as followers of Jesus, they found themselves compelled to enlarge the borders of their personal lives and churches through the persistent practice of personal and corporate evangelism.

Jesus promised His disciples that the church would be His witness in an ever-expanding circle of influence around the world. As Acts 1:8 states, "But you will receive power when the Holy Spirit comes on you; and you will be my witnesses in Jerusalem, and in all Judea and Samaria, and to the ends of the earth." These words of Jesus aren't so much a command (you shall) as a promise (you will). For the Holy Spirit transforms the command of the Great Commission (go into all the world and proclaim the Gospel) into a promise fulfilled in our lives by His power.

By His Power Alone

Understanding the power of the Holy Spirit is the key to experiencing the personal transformation that overflows into a life of fruitful witness. As the late Henrietta Mears said, "I believe that it is impossible for any Christian to be effective in either his life or in his service unless he is filled with the Holy Spirit who is God's only provision of power."

What is the Spirit-filled life? Very simply, it is the Christ-directed, Christ-centered, Christ-filled life by which Christ lives His life in and through us by the power of the Holy Spirit. The Scriptures command every Christian to "be filled with the Spirit" (Ephesians 5:18). This means that we are to allow Jesus to take His rightful place in our lives "on the throne," as our "master affection," first priority, and first love. As Jesus resides on the throne, He fills us with Himself and begins the process of displacing all that would challenge His kingship in our lives. As He is seated on the throne, we have the privilege of drawing on His infinite resources, His love, mercy, power, and forgiveness moment by moment as a way of life. Only then are we able to meet life's opportunities and challenges in His power.

Since the Holy Spirit came to make Jesus a living reality in our daily experience (John 16:14, 15), as we are filled with the Holy Spirit by means of our contact with Scripture, the Lord Jesus transforms our character, motivations, and goals to conform with His.

Transformed Ambassadors

Consider for a moment the difference the Holy Spirit made in the lives of the disciples after Jesus' ascension. He took a band of fearful and defeated believers and transformed them into a group of bold and fruitful evangelists, ready and willing to risk their lives for the cause of the Gospel.

In a similar way, the Holy Spirit wants to take us, fearful and reluctant ambassadors that we sometimes are, and transform us into fishers of men.

As we walk with Him in the Spirit's power, our sight, sensitivities, and actions are transformed. We will begin to see the lost as Jesus saw them: as helpless sheep without a shepherd. We will begin to feel toward the lost as Jesus felt toward them: moved with compassion. We will begin to act toward the lost as Jesus acted toward them: compassionately meeting their needs while sensitively and boldly sharing the Gospel (Matthew 9:35–38). Growing in Him is a matter of developing the eyes and heart of His ambassador.

Spiritual Growth Results From Evangelism

Have you ever had days when you didn't feel like sharing your faith, when you didn't feel changed or especially grateful? I certainly have. But should we actively share our faith, even when it's inconvenient or we don't feel like it?

While we saw from the examples of Matthew, Philip, and others that evangelism is often the spontaneous overflow of a transformed life, the Scriptures also tell us to be prepared to share the Gospel "in season and *out of season*" (2 Timothy 4:2, italics added) and to "endure hardship, do the work of an evangelist, discharge all the duties of your ministry" (2 Timothy 4:5).

In other words, we shouldn't be surprised when evangelism is difficult and inconvenient, or even "out of season." Even as we walk in the power of the Holy Spirit, the practice of personal evangelism will require our diligent effort and rigorous personal discipline. As Paul described the effort that went into his ministry, "To this end I labor, struggling with all his energy, which so powerfully works in me" (Colossians 1:29).

The Work of an Evangelist

If I were to ask you to list some of the spiritual disciplines, prayer, Bible study, fasting, and Scripture memory would quickly come to mind. Evangelism probably would not make the list. But this isn't all that surprising.

The role of accountability and discipline in the Christian life in general and evangelism in particular is often misunderstood. By spiritual discipline I mean those activities that we voluntarily put in our schedule to enhance our relationship with Jesus and service for Him. Spiritual disciplines broaden our comfort zone, that range of activity we feel comfortable in doing. Properly understood, spiritual disciplines are the *result* of our Spirit-filled walk and the Spirit's *means* of drawing us closer to Jesus.

While our spiritual growth provides us with the motivation and power for sharing our faith, so the practice of sharing our faith as a spiritual discipline accelerates our spiritual growth. Let me explain.

Often our practice of a spiritual discipline is the very means the Spirit uses to make that discipline a natural part of our lives. Why is this? Because the more I practice something, the more natural I feel doing it, and the more confident I become in that area of my life.

For instance, few of us would say that the daily practice of persistent, intercessory prayer is a natural part of our lives. But the more we discipline ourselves to set aside time to pray, the more natural prayer will feel. The more natural I feel praying, the more I will want to pray. And, of course, the more we practice prayer, the more we will see specific answers to prayer. Then we will be motivated to pray even more.

The Holy Spirit, working through the Word, is the Author of this cycle of growth overflowing into discipline, which overflows into more growth. When practiced in the power of the Holy Spirit, the disciplines then are aids, not obstructions, to our spiritual growth. Evangelism is no exception.

The Spiritual Disciplines in Practice

One of my warmest recollections as a new believer is spending a beautiful June evening outdoors talking with five of my hometown friends. We had all been away at college for most of the year and were meeting to catch up on the latest news. I had no idea that by the time the evening was through, I would be thankful to God for using my practice of some spiritual disciplines to bear fruit in my own life and in the lives of my friends.

Though I had been a believer for only a few months, a friend had encouraged me to begin putting some of the spiritual disciplines into my schedule. So I had begun studying and memorizing the Scriptures and praying regularly for each of my friends with the hope that I could soon tell each of them about Christ.

As the evening progressed and the conversation turned to some of the major events in each of our personal lives, I realized that God was arranging the opportunity for me to apply the fruit of these spiritual disciplines in a "live" situation. The time seemed right to share my testimony and the Gospel. In the midst of my awkwardness and fear, I shared what Jesus had done in my life.

Armed with the fruit of these disciplines (a few verses memorized, a very basic knowledge of the Scriptures, and the confidence that comes from time logged in prayer), I was able to communicate my testimony and give each of my friends an opportunity to hear the Gospel. The conversation was difficult and awkward at times, but God used this experience in a mighty way. It led to many more conversations about Jesus and the eventual conversion of one friend and his wife.

But this time was also fruitful in terms of my own growth. That evening I had a deep sense of God's supernatural presence, even in the midst of persistent ridicule and questions I couldn't answer. By the end of the evening I had a much deeper appreciation of what God had done in my own life through the Gospel. I was able to see for the first time how radically different I was because Jesus was now in my life. I tasted the goodness of God toward me and felt, albeit to a limited degree, the mercy and love God feels toward those who don't yet know Him. In short, I became more aware of the ability of Jesus to change lives and especially my life, which continues to need changing.

This was a time of accelerated growth for me. God had used the spiritual disciplines of prayer, Bible study, and memorization not only to draw me closer to Himself but also to prepare me for an evangelistic experience that contributed greatly to my growth as a new believer.

But why does an experience like this accelerate our spiritual growth? It's because some powerful principles of growth are at work. Let's take a look at some of these principles of spiritual growth.

Principle #1: The Fruit Is at the End of the Limb

That evening I realized that God was leading me to step out on the end of the limb. I would have to venture outside my comfort zone and overcome my fear of sharing the Gospel. But as I took my first step, I found the footing firm and a faithful God upholding me by the Spirit's power.

As John Greenleaf Whittier's verse goes:

> Nothing before, nothing behind,
>   The steps of Faith
> Fall on the seeming void, and find
>   The rock beneath.[3]

Or, as one author put it, "The Spirit is not a guide and a helper for those on a straight way perfectly able to manage on their own. He comes to assist men caught up in the thick of battle, and tried beyond their strength."[4] Evangelism, if nothing else, is a matter of "getting caught up in the thick of battle," and for me that evening it was surely an experience that "tried me beyond my strength."

But this is a good place to be, because sharing our faith puts us where Jesus is working. It puts us in the midst of the spiritual battle raging over men's and women's souls. It puts us where God can use us in the lives of others. It puts us where we can and must draw upon His infinite resources. In short, it puts us right where God wants us, and that will always be the best place to grow.

Principle # 2: A Kite Flies Best Against the Wind

Just as the resistance of wind helps a kite or plane become airborne, so God uses opposition (the resistance of people or circumstances) to enhance our spiritual growth.

The principle that opposition stimulates growth is not only true in the spiritual realm but in the physical realm as well.

Japanese farmers have discovered the truth of "stress-induced growth" in their pursuit of growing stronger and larger vegetables. Experimenting with a technique called "Mechanically Induced Stress," these farmers poked the vegetables with brooms before transplanting them in greenhouses. Researchers in the United States, Great Britain, and Japan shake and bend plants a few minutes a day, bringing positive results. Cauliflower, lettuce, and celery have grown sturdier than those plants left alone.

The parallels to our spiritual growth are obvious. God uses trials (stress) in our lives to draw us closer to Himself and conform our character to the image of Christ (James 1:2–4; Romans 5:3–5). Yes, the character of Christ is best produced in us as we walk against the wind. In fact, we might even say that we must walk into the prevailing wind of opposition if the development of our character is to get off the ground.

Of course, nothing exposes us to opposition more than being involved in evangelism. That summer evening I found my words meeting resistance. I was a minority of one, walking alone, against the wind.

Evangelistic situations like this produce healthy stress, the kind of stress that requires us to trust in the Holy Spirit for boldness, sensitivity, and perseverance. Just as muscles need exercising, so our "faith muscles" need exercise, extension, and exertion to grow strong. As the old saying goes, "Man's extremity is God's opportunity." The man or woman in the midst of spiritual battle will be driven to his or her knees in an attitude of prayerful, humble dependence. This is a wonderful place to grow.

Principle #3: We Resemble What We Focus Upon

In a recent study at the University of Michigan, researchers found scientific evidence for the widely held belief that couples actually begin to look alike after years of marriage. People were shown two dozen pictures of individual newlyweds and two dozen pictures of the same people twenty-five years later. They were then asked to match the men and women who they thought most closely resembled each other.

The young couples showed only chance resemblance to each other, but those judging the pictures saw a marked resemblance in the older couples. The authors of the study concluded that people unconsciously mimic the facial expressions of their spouses.

The application to the spiritual dimension of life is profound. We are most likely to become like the person we gaze upon. And so the author of Hebrews encourages us to "fix our eyes on Jesus" (Hebrews 12:2), and Paul reminds us that as we focus on the Lord, we will "with unveiled faces all reflect the Lord's glory . . . which comes from the Lord, who is the Spirit" (2 Corinthians 3:18).

The application to evangelism is also profound. The practice of personal evangelism exposes us to the displacement principle of growth. Evangelism focuses us on Jesus, and the more we focus on Him, the less room we have in our lives for the competing voices of the world, flesh, and devil. As we focus on Jesus, we are brought, in Chalmers' words, "under the mastery of one great and dominant affection."

As Paul states in the sixth verse of Philemon, "I pray that you may be active in sharing your faith, so that you will have a full understanding of every good thing we have in Christ."

If evangelism does nothing else, it focuses on the Lord Jesus Christ as our strength for the moment and the source of eternal life for the lost. Indeed, my speaking the Gospel actually ministers to me as well. As I tell of His love, I cannot help but more deeply appreciate His love in my own life. As I tell of His holiness, I cannot help but sense how desperately I need His daily grace and power to overcome sin. As I tell of His resurrection, I am reminded that today the risen Jesus is alive and more than able to meet my need by His resurrection power.

We could go on recounting how evangelism refreshes and focuses the evangelist on the life-changing power of Jesus. Suffice it to say that, as we practice evangelism, we come away with a greater personal understanding of "every good thing we have in Christ."

Our Foundation for Daily Growth

Involvement in personal evangelism puts us in touch with these powerful principles of spiritual growth, and, as a result, we are never the same. As we share our faith, the borders of our hearts are enlarged, enabling us to receive even more blessing from the Lord. Our wayward wills are straightened so that we might better walk in the paths of righteousness. Our blurred vision is cleared that we might better see "the light of the gospel of the glory of Christ, who is the image of God" (2 Corinthians 4:4).

What greater foundation for daily growth could anyone have than the Gospel itself? We are objects of His love and concern. We are on the cutting edge of God at work in the world. We are a people of great privilege and destiny. We are deeply loved. We have been given eternally significant work, but we have eternally significant power available in

God's grace. We are being changed from the inside out by that power.

As we are involved in personal evangelism, we find ourselves taking steps of faith that catch us up, yes, even against the wind, in God's great plans to reach the world through His transformed ambassadors.

Discussion Questions

1. Why is it essential to walk in the power of the Holy Spirit as we share our faith? How can we do that?

2. What would result in our lives if we didn't walk by the Spirit's power as we witnessed? Can you recall a witnessing experience when you walked in your own power?

3. What role does God's Word play in our spiritual growth?

4. Must we reach a certain level of spirituality before we begin to share our faith? Why or why not?

5. Why is evangelism so hard to practice, even compared with other spiritual disciplines?

6. Think back to an effective witness you once gave. To what do you attribute that effectiveness?

7. Have times of spiritual dryness in your life been times of little or no witnessing? What turns that around?

8. Why is faith strengthened by witnessing?

9. How much do you look like Jesus?

3
The Art of Friendship

Jerry and Mary White

Everyone needs friends. Most people want friends. But not everyone knows how to win and keep friends. Friendship is fundamental to all human relationships. Things get done in life more by relationships than by conflicts and arguments. But what underlies a real friendship? What makes it work?

Some people seem to find dozens of friends, moving almost effortlessly among close relationships. Others seem to be perpetually lonely, stumbling at most attempts to develop deep friendships. Part of this difference is attributed to personality. But personality alone does not make for genuine friendships. Making friends is truly an art—an art that can be learned.

Since friendship is common to all human interaction, it is one of the primary doors into the lives of nonbelievers.

Confrontational witnessing fails with many people—even offending and turning them against the Gospel. Friendship is a real bridge. But many of us find it difficult to develop these friendships.

Jim and Karen Robinson dropped their two children at the church for a Saturday outing with young people. Instead of going home and plunging into the weekend chores, they drove to a coffee shop for breakfast. They were obviously troubled and said very little as they were served. Finally Karen said, "Jim, I just can't understand it. We've known Al and Bonnie for eight years. I was certain they would at least accept our invitation to discuss having a Bible study."

"Me, too. But I'm just as puzzled that the Carsons and the Parks turned me down flat. We've got a big zero!"

"But why, Jim? We've never pushed our Christianity on them. They acted as if we were strangers when we asked them to our home."

"I really don't understand it. We followed the pastor's instructions to the letter. We listed our friends. We prayed for them. We contacted each of them personally and invited them for dessert at our house. We were honest and explained that we wanted to organize a four-week investigative Bible study and asked them to consider it. We promised there would be no pressure and that they could decide after the first get-together if they wanted to join the study. But everyone made excuses—some of them pretty lame ones, too."

"You know, I've sensed a coolness in several of the wives over the last two years."

"It makes me wonder, Karen, if they really are our friends anymore. When was the last time we did anything with them socially? Over a year ago, wasn't it?"

Jim and Karen analyzed and talked for almost an hour. They finally concluded that their friendship with these nonbelieving neighbors had died long ago and they had not known it. They went on thinking they were still friends but did nothing to maintain or build the relationships. A brief look at their history will reveal some of what happened.

Jim was an up-and-coming businessman. He was talented and ambitious. He and Karen were socially active both in his company and in their neighborhood. A week rarely went by when they did not entertain and attend some social function. They were bright spots in the party circle. Karen was active in community affairs, women's concern groups, and the school PTA.

When they were first married, they did not regularly attend church but went occasionally at Christmas and Easter. They considered themselves religious in a private way. Jim's background was nonreligious. Karen came from a churchgoing, believing family. She became a Christian as a teenager but abandoned any type of Christian practice when she was in college.

As time passed, Karen became disturbed at the quickening pace of their life-style and the absence of God from any part of it. She and Jim argued more and enjoyed each other less. Finally they decided to start attending church again. After a few months, Jim recognized his need for Christ and accepted Christ as his Savior. Karen recommitted her life to Christ at the same time.

Then their entire lives underwent radical changes. Ambitions assumed a biblical perspective. Their marriage strengthened. Their social life in the party world died. They began to focus on spiritual growth, their family, and church activities.

All the change was largely for the best. But what they didn't see was the subtle separation taking place between themselves and longtime friends. They witnessed to them openly. They turned down party invitations. They withdrew from most nonspiritual activities. They wrapped themselves into a Christian cocoon, isolated from meaningful outside relationships.

At the coffee shop it dawned on them that they had placed themselves in Christian isolation. They had lost their personal influence on the world. They were cheered on by Christians. They shared their testimonies, and they studied the Bible. They grew spiritually, but they climbed out of the world and pulled the ladder up after them. Their link with the past broke, and their friends no longer listened to them.

From Jewish history and practice, we recall that the Jews could not even eat with the Gentiles, much less be friends. Fortunately, Jesus Christ Himself broke the ancient Jewish pattern of separation and paved the way for a new set of relationships with non-Christians. Jesus was accused of being "a friend of tax collectors and 'sinners' " (Luke 7:34). When He was attacked for eating and drinking with these tax collectors and sinners, He answered, "It is not the healthy who need a doctor, but the sick. I have not come to call the righteous, but sinners to repentance" (Luke 5:31, 32). Jesus set a new pattern in His ministry of relating to the unbeliever. He didn't avoid believers, but His relationships were not exclusively with them.

Jesus intends for us to develop relationships with non-Christians in the normal course of our lives. How else can we be light and salt in our work, neighborhoods, and society? Our relationships must go beyond preaching or telling the Gospel once, and then breaking the relationship if there is no response. We must stick with our friends over a period of time to help them see the difference Christ makes in our lives.

Should we be friends with non-Christians? Yes. We are under obligation to search them out and befriend them as Christ would have done.

But how? Even if we want to befriend them, we often

run up against obstacles which keep us from developing close friendships with nonbelievers.

Stumbling Blocks

The hindrances are few in number but great in their effect. Significant differences do exist between believers and nonbelievers. They approach life from different viewpoints. In forming and keeping friendships, key elements of communication may not be there.

A lack of common spiritual experience and dimension hinders totally open communication. We cannot easily share what really grips our hearts and minds in our walk with Christ. As we interact with non-Christians, we often find that the most important issues of our lives are not the same as theirs.

We may engage in different life-styles and interest patterns. A high percentage of many Christians' optional activities involves meetings with the church and relationships with other Christians. Although we need to grow through fellowship, we must guard against creating different worlds that never touch each other. Christians and non-Christians simply do not engage in many overlapping areas of activities.

Christians and non-Christians are not always naturally attracted to one another. Their life-style may turn us off. Or ours may turn them off. Even conversation can dry up if we've allowed ourselves to grow out of touch with concerns outside Christian circles. Unless we seek out and maintain friendships with non-Christians, we can too easily slide into the dangerous attitude of complacency, which says, "I'll get along with you if I have to, but don't encroach on my personal space."

Our motives for developing a friendship are too often evangelistic in nature. Non-Christians see through these motives. A conditional, recruiting friendship rarely lives long. Who wants to be a notch on a spiritual gun? But what can we do about this? How can we be a true friend without sharing Jesus Christ, the most important part of our lives?

We can't. But we can clarify and improve our motives. And we can get over the hurdles that separate us from our non-Christian friends.

Understanding Friendship

We each have in our minds the image of the ideal friend. That image colors all our thinking about making friends. Most often that image results from our experiences—good and bad—and the type of personality we possess. Yet every person's image is different. Thus we each impose differing expectations on our friendship.

As we consider building friendships with our unbelieving friends, it is helpful to understand the most critical elements in forming lasting and rewarding friendships. These elements apply to both Christian and non-Christian friendships. Use the "friendship arch" below as a guide for your friendships.

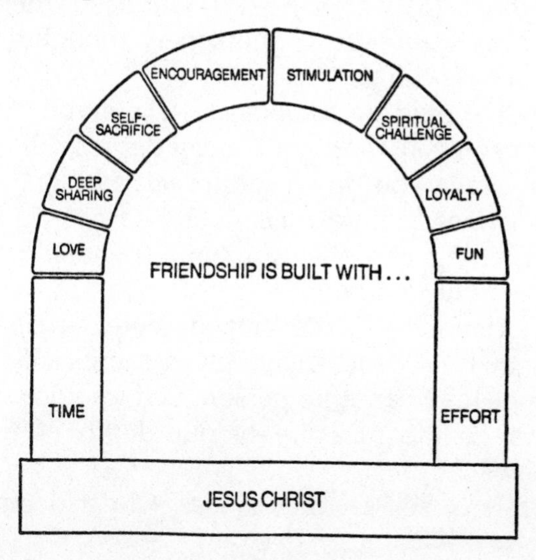

In surveys for the book *Friends and Friendships,* people overwhelmingly said that the characteristic they valued most in a friend was *loyalty*. We all want friends we can trust and rely on. No one wants a fair-weather friend who disappears at the first sign of trouble or personal inconvenience. The false friends of Proverbs 19:4–7 "are nowhere to be found." Loyalty means keeping confidences, defending your friend, and giving support in time of adversity.

The next characteristic of a good friend is *sharing deeply*. People want to share their hearts and to receive understanding in return. The elements are listening, wise speech, and true acceptance.

People also want friends who are *fun to be with*. This often means common interests: tennis, reading, sewing, hiking, decorating, cars, gardening. Think of creative things to do together: plays, sports, a spontaneous birthday party, a weekend away, a surprise work party to paint a friend's garage.

A friendship should be *stimulating*. No one wants boring relationships. "As iron sharpens iron, so one man sharpens another" (Proverbs 27:17). We need friends who challenge us, cause us to think new thoughts, awaken interest in new things.

A friend should be *encouraging*. Have you ever spent time with someone and gone away depressed? A friendship that drags you down cannot survive long. Encouragement comes in little ways: words, a note, a flower, a gift, a listening ear. We want our friendship to be an encouragement to others.

Once a friendship has developed, there is a *self-sacrificing* element to it. A true friend gives sacrificially to meet pressing needs of another person. Self-sacrifice instead of selfishness is the measure of our depth of friendship (Philippians 2:4).

The basis of self-sacrifice is *love*. Christ demonstrated

this *agape* love—unconditional love with no thought of repayment. Without real love there is no real friendship. People will sense whether there is that kind of love underlying the friendship.

Finally, the friendship should be *spiritually challenging*. Even with non-Christians there is a spiritual element. However, the spiritual element is not just religious jargon or talk but real-life issues that matter. For the believer, that includes a life in Christ. If a friendship is well founded, there will be openness in every area, including the spiritual.

Then time and effort are necessary to build these roots of friendship. For the believer, Jesus Christ is the foundation and motive for every relationship.

But you may say, "This kind of relationship is all-consuming." Not every relationship has all these characteristics present in full measure. There are many levels of friendship in real life. The figure on page 56 shows levels of friendships. We develop hundreds of acquaintances across the years. From these, many casual friends develop. We can maintain fifty to one hundred casual friends—people whose names we know, people we see from time to time but rarely see socially or on a personal basis.

Out of these many casual friends come some *close* friends. We see these friends frequently and share much of our lives with them. They include people in our extended family, "associates" from work, civic groups, and church, as well as others whom we choose as "personal" friends. People can maintain ten to twenty close friends exclusive of family.

Finally, we can maintain a small number of *intimate* friends who meet most of the characteristics described earlier. We estimate only about three to five intimate friends in a lifetime. Truly intimate friends are a rare commodity.

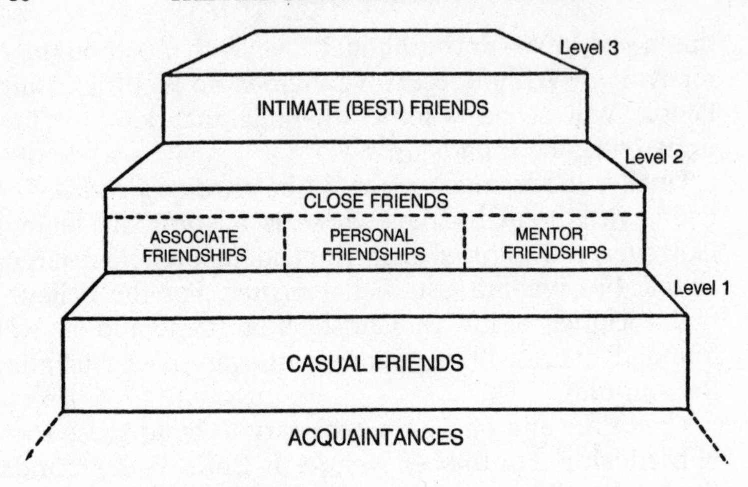

Can nonbelievers come into these patterns? They certainly can.

Making Friends With Non-Christians

Friendships with non-Christians keep us in touch with reality. The majority of the world is non-Christian. The reclusive life in a Christian environment is unknown to most unbelievers, and they need special sight to see the ultimate reality of the Christian life. Non-Christians need a keyhole to look through. Perhaps your life and friendship could be that special keyhole.

Clarify your motives. Christians are often caught in a dilemma. We can pursue a meaningful friendship with a non-Christian without envisioning their coming to Christ, yet as we mentioned above, evangelistic motives can be a stumbling block to that same meaningful friendship. Clarifying our motives will help to resolve this dilemma.

We must distinguish between evangelism *in the course of* friendship and friendship *for the purpose of* evangelism. We cannot deny our inner drive and disobey Christ's specific command to evangelize. In some sense it is part of any relationship with non-Christians, and our life in Christ must affect that relationship. We cannot suppress who and what we are.

Our motive in developing a friendship with a non-Christian, however, *includes* evangelism, but it should not be *only* for evangelism. We love our friends for many reasons. As we love them, we demonstrate it by sharing the most significant issue of our lives: Jesus Christ. In a true friendship, they will respect that which means so much to us.

The problem arises when the friendship is motivated only by evangelism, and our friends sense it. They feel manipulated.

In his fine book *Life-Style Evangelism*, Dr. Joseph C. Aldrich says, "Witness begins with *presence*, moves to *proclamation*, and then on to *persuasion*."[1] He describes presence as the flavor or music of our lives that attracts others to God. Proclamation is the direct presentation of the Gospel message. Persuasion is the encouragement to make a final decision to become a Christian.

In his book *Evangelism as a Lifestyle*, Jim Petersen emphasizes that we must be willing to emerge from our Christian isolation and enter the arena where the non-Christian lives:

> Such isolation has a destructive effect on a local body of Christians, as well as destroying our communication with the lost. Christians who keep to themselves, who do not experience a continuing influx of people just arriving from the dominion of darkness, soon surround themselves with their own subculture. Receiving no feedback from people fresh from the world, they forget what it's like out there. Peculiar

> language codes, behavioral patterns, and communication techniques emerge that only have meaning for insiders. As such, a local body becomes increasingly ingrown. Eventually, communication with the man on the street is impossible.[2]

As we relate outwardly to the lost, we must do so not just out of obligation but out of real love for others. God will honor that motive for friendship. Non-Christians will read and accept that motive without suspicion.

Decide to do it. We believe that expanding your friendship circle to include non-Christians requires a definite decision. It does not just happen. As it takes conscious effort to develop a Christian friendship, so it also takes a conscious decision and effort to pursue a non-Christian friendship. It may mean joining activities where you will find non-Christians.

Find friends in the ordinary course of life and work. Imagine yourself walking down a busy sidewalk. A stranger stops you and asks, "Pardon me, but would you consider being my friend?" Your mind runs through a series of replies from *Why?* to *Don't bother me.* You no doubt think, *What an odd way to get a friend.* That is no way to find a friend, Christian or non-Christian.

God placed you in a unique set of circumstances in which you can find many sources of non-Christian relationships. Think of these natural settings. The past may include high school and college, your old neighborhood, family—aunts, uncles, cousins—and former jobs.

Perhaps your present circumstances include neighbors, co-workers and professional colleagues, club members, relatives and in-laws, parents of your children's friends, or people you meet at school functions. Future situations might bring new neighbors, extended family through your children's marriages, and new co-workers.

Don't let old friendships die. They are irreplaceable. We have seen several of those casual friendships of fifteen and twenty years in the past redevelop as paths cross and needs change. Most still remain at the casual level. Some are individual with one of us, and some friendships involve us as a couple. Keep some of those people on your Christmas card list and see if you can renew friendships.

Over the years I have made a concerted effort to maintain many relationships of the past. I regularly call and see my fifth-grade teacher and my high school history teacher. For several years I have pursued a particular high school acquaintance who experienced great public popularity, then fell into obscurity. I used to visit one childhood friend regularly when he was in prison. I looked him up several times in later years. Anyone can make friendship overtures to acquaintances from the past.

Be where non-Christian friendships can develop. Although we make initial contacts at work or across the fence, seldom do the friendships develop there. They need a more sociable environment. In their home or yours, at a sports event or party, in a community club or on a fishing trip—be there. Your presence opens doors. Have you noticed how different the conversation will be at a company picnic compared with the office or shop? The relaxed atmosphere puts people at ease and produces a good climate for friendship.

In my years in the air force, I deliberately entered activities in which I could enjoy social interaction with non-Christians. I frequently played on fast-pitch softball teams. I played with and coached an air force academy faculty volleyball team. I played handball with other faculty members. We made department socials a priority. We felt that these activities were a key to our non-Christian friendships.

Don't hide your Christianity. Fly your flag early. This does not mean a verbal witness the first time you are introduced. But as you talk, the fact that you attend church, read your Bible, or have religious beliefs should emerge naturally over a period of time.

A fellow faculty member at the air force academy and I had known each other since 1962. In the first months of our acquaintance, he asked some advice on teaching Sunday school at the base chapel, although he was not a Christian. This led to occasional religious discussions over the next eight years. In 1975 he called and asked to see me. He was deeply troubled over an incident with his son and wanted prayer. A few days later, he received Christ. Thirteen years of casual friendship were part of God's plan of reaching him. But if my Christianity had been hidden, he never would have asked the initial question in 1962.

Look for common interests or goals. A friendship often grows around something like a pearl around a grain of sand. Sports, children, schools, professional development, sewing, gardening, politics—each of these could be a starting point. If you have to, broaden your interests. Observe what people enjoy and ask them about it. Talk about what you enjoy. When you strike that common chord, you will both know it.

Make friends with people you like. Here again, we are discussing friendship, not just evangelism. Ask God to develop in you a love for people. Display your interest in them and be a magnet to draw them to God. We all find ourselves drawn to certain people for various reasons. Use that attraction as a basis for friendship.

Use your home. Your home reveals who you are more than any other environment. Bring people into that part of your life. They will see your books, your children, the kind of furniture you like, your hobbies, your tastes, and your relationships. They'll absorb all of this information and decide whether or not they like you or want to pursue a friendship with you. And you may receive an invitation to their home, which will help you make the same decisions.

Pray for keys to friendship. A friendship seldom develops

around every aspect of our lives; usually two or three common interests bring us together and generate topics of conversation. Pray that you will observe these keys and be able to pursue them. Ask God to make you sensitive to others' interests and needs, and pray that they will be responsive to your overtures of friendship. And, of course, ask God to make Christ evident to them through your life.

Look for special needs. At certain times of life people are more eager for friends than at others: when they are new to a city or job, when a divorce occurs, when a teenager gets into trouble, when the job begins to disintegrate, or when illness strikes. If we remain alert, our opportunity to develop the friendship may come through that specific need.

Be patient—don't force the friendship. A certain tentativeness characterizes the initial stages of a friendship. If things move too fast, the friendship can be smothered. Remember that everyone has other friendships and relationships that must be maintained. They will not abandon everything to pursue a friendship at a casual pace; this allows plenty of time and space for healthy communication. Ask God for wisdom in how quickly or slowly to pursue the friendship.

Accept them as they are. Don't try to change new friends. You want them to accept you as you are—a believer in Christ. You need to communicate the same acceptance to them, regardless of what they do. Keep in mind Thoreau's remark, "The most I can do for my friend is simply to be his friend" (*Journal*, February 7, 1841).

How to Be Attractive to Others

The mystery of human attraction continues to puzzle scientists and psychologists. The magnetism between two distinct personalities defies description both in romance and in friendship. All the computer analysis in the world will never solve the matching chemistry between two human personalities, because the most unusual friendship can develop in spite of disparities in personality and interests. Yet certain characteristics play a significant part in *initial* attraction, particularly between believers and unbelievers.

Have you ever noticed how some people possess a charisma that draws people to them? Some people have it and some don't. But as you go beyond the issues of personality, some common threads of attraction begin to emerge.

Inevitably, material success and social status stimulate initial attraction, if for no other reason than vicarious fascination. But if these are not backed up by an attractive person underneath, the attraction will quickly fade. These factors can be useful only in whetting someone's interest. The quality of an individual life is what really counts.

Most of us have little control over success and status anyway. We can focus on becoming more attractive to non-Christians, however, no matter what our position in life, by striving to develop the following characteristics.

Christlikeness. "When they saw the courage of Peter and John and realized that they were unschooled, ordinary men, they were astonished and they took note that these men had been with Jesus" (Acts 4:13). We become like the person we spend the most time with. As we spend time with Jesus, we become like Him, and people sense it. All our efforts to attract others are worthless if Jesus Christ is not honored in the process. The aroma of Christ in us attracts people in a way that surpasses all others.

This subject, which could really be a separate book, underlies all other issues. But to be Christlike we must do those things that build Christlikeness: a personal devotional life, obedience to His Word, study of His Word, and fellowship with other Christians. Do people see a difference in your life? Do they observe you and take note that you have been with Jesus? This is the master magnet of a truly attractive life. Build it at all costs.

Godly response to suffering. No one wants to suffer, yet most of us will suffer physically or emotionally in some way in the next few years. What response will characterize your life then? Bitterness? Complaints? Despair? Joy? Patience? Whatever your response, people will notice it. They often watch with morbid fascination as another person struggles through the deeper problems of life. The spectacle of suffering is a magnet.

If you respond in a godly way to your sufferings and trials, non-Christians will take note and privately wonder why. Then, as they face personal suffering, they may turn to you as a source of help. Perhaps even without a problem of their own, they may ask why your response was different. As you struggle in your suffering, remember that your life is being transformed into a magnet that draws people to you and to God. Let God use you in a special way in times of distress.

Honesty. In a world where honesty and ethics often take a backseat to expediency and opportunity, a truly honest person stands out above the crowd. The way we speak, work, or do business makes a definite impression on people. As people grapple with issues of ethics in their work, others watch how they respond, fully expecting them to opt for their own selfish interests when opportunity exists. A Christian who refuses to lie, stretch the truth, or falsify a document certainly attracts notice. Though some will be turned off by honesty because they don't want to face their own guilt, others will be drawn to it in respect and admiration.

Generosity. People love a generous person. One who gives time, money, or help will always attract friends. Adopt a Christlike, giving spirit, and you will be rewarded with the pleasure of helping others as well as with the satisfaction of drawing others to you.

Competence. Not everyone will succeed spectacularly, but everyone can achieve a measure of success by performing competently at an appropriate level of ability. A successful person always wields an influence in some circle of people, whether that person is a wife with a knack for decorating, a mechanic who can fix anything, an engineer who can see through problems, a student who gets high grades, a salesman who excels in selling, or a dependable and responsible manager. As we develop competence in our tasks at work, in the home, or even in our hobbies, we attract people who come to us out of respect, for our instruction and help.

No matter what you do, if you dedicate it to the Lord and perform it to the best of your ability, you will attract others.

A strong marriage. As marriages crumble around us, the stable, happy marriage shines like a spotlight on a black night. As non-Christians struggle in their marriages, they grope for answers but rarely know where to turn. Our society's confusion about the family clouds the issue even more. A truly happy couple seems unique.

Is your marriage truly attractive? Can people see contrasts to the world's standards in your marriage? They should. If they do, you will attract even non-Christians and open the door to a friendship. Others long to know the secret to a happy marriage. Share your secret with them.

Close and loving family bonds. Ask parents in their forties about their children, and you will probably strike a sensitive area. Few people, Christian or non-Christian, escape the hazards and hassles of raising teenagers. If your family grapples successfully with the issues of raising children in both younger and teen years, you will have a significant platform for attracting others.

Results speak louder than sermons. As you talk with

non-Christians, the issue of children will probably open lines of communication. But telling is insufficient. People need to see and relate to your family. Invite them to your home and let them observe you firsthand. No family is perfect, but if you have tried to apply biblical principles in raising your children, chances are others will notice a difference in your home. Allow your family to attract non-Christians.

We can and should build friendships with non-Christians. Guard against becoming hermit Christians, and instead respond to the great need and opportunity to be Christ's man or woman in the midst of a secular world. May God grant us the heart and vision to befriend the lost of the world and to befriend each other as we draw closer to Him.

Discussion Questions

1. How many non-Christian friends do you have?

2. With whom among your circle of acquaintances could you begin to develop a friendship?

3. What is the proper motivation for developing friendships with non-Christians? What is the improper motivation?

4. What is the difference between "evangelism in the course of friendship" and "friendship for the purpose of evangelism"?

5. Have you ever been someone else's "project"? How did you feel?

6. How often do you have non-Christians into your home? What kinds of events could you hold in your home to which you could invite non-Christians?

7. What does it take to respond in a godly way to suffering? How well do you do that? *See* Acts 4:18–20, 29–31; 5:40, 41; 1 Peter 1:6, 7.

8. Does the discussion of characteristics such as honesty, generosity, a strong marriage, and Christlikeness make you feel inadequate? How does forgiveness help you deal with such feelings? How can an open attitude toward your own failings actually open a door for a witness?

9. In which of the above areas (honesty, generosity, etc.) do you need to work?

4
The Art of Showing Love

Joseph C. Aldrich

Arms wrapped around his trusty teddy bear, the young lad tried to be brave. But a horrendous lightning storm melted his bravery and sent him packing down the hall to snuggle up with Mom and Dad.

From the safety of his snuggle he announced, "Daddy, I'm afraid."

"No need to be afraid," his daddy assured him. "God is with us."

"I know that, Dad," he replied. "But right now I need someone with skin on."

So does your neighbor. The song says it well.

"Don't tell me what a friend I have in Jesus 'til you show me what a friend I have in you."

If you've got skin on, you can be a friend, because God still wraps ideas in people. Making truth live in the lives of people is His specialty. The Living Word became flesh, and His generation saw His glory. "His life," John tells us, "is the light" (John 1:5 TLB). It still is. Yes, His life is still the light. That life, incarnated through you and me, continues to be the light.

"Let your light shine before men," instructed the Living Word, "that they may see your good deeds . . ." (Matthew 5:16). Note that the Lord invites the nonbeliever to look, not listen.

So a Christian attorney is not simply an attorney; he's God's light-bearer in the courtroom to demonstrate how a God-flavored lawyer relates to the judge and jury. A secretary shines as a light when she brings the beauty of a Christ-filled life to the realities of the corporate world. Taking a meal to an ailing neighbor also flips the light switch.

So what do people see when they see the light? Good deeds? Isaiah records an answer to that question. God reminds us that our light rises like the morning sun, our righteousness goes before us, and the glory of God becomes our rear guard when we do things like:

clothing the naked
releasing those imprisoned
feeding the hungry
caring for our senior citizens
and so on (*see* Isaiah 58)

Our light shines when we do as the early church did. Luke's account records them selling, giving, worshiping, sacrificing, and serving with a joyful spirit. Is it any wonder they were "enjoying the favor of all the people"? Or that God "added to their number daily those who were being saved" (Acts 2:47)?

Luke sandwiched a description of the powerful apostolic preaching between two interesting "bookends."

Bookend One: Unity + Individual Sacrifice and Generosity

"All the believers were one in heart and mind. No one claimed that any of his possessions was his own, but they shared everything they had" (Acts 4:32).

Description of the impact: "With great power the apostles continued to testify to the resurrection of the Lord Jesus, and much grace was upon them all" (Acts 4:33).

Bookend Two: Corporate Generosity

"There were no needy persons among them. For from time to time those who owned lands or houses sold them, brought the money from the sales and put it at the apostles' feet, and it was distributed to anyone as he had need" (Acts 4:34, 35).

The sacrificial, loving life-style of the believers enhanced, illustrated, and empowered the apostolic proclamation. The nonbelievers were amazed at the early Christians' stewardship of resources. Human nature hoards when things get tough. Not these Christians! Their visible unity and generosity were remarkable, convincing, and an answer to Christ's high priestly prayer. We shouldn't be surprised at the response. Remember that on the eve of His betrayal, Jesus prayed that believers would be united so the world would know God loved them (John 17).

It bears repeating: "And the Lord added to their number daily those who were being saved" (Acts 2:47).

Certainly God's communication strategy involves both the visualization and verbalization of truth! When love is felt, someone has said, the message is heard. So what does it mean to love?

In the broadest sense, to love is to be a God-flavored person. It is to think, act, and respond within the boundary conditions of God's character. The redemptive person reveals the universals of God's character through the particulars of everyday life. Like Christ, we are called to make visible the invisible God through our attitudes, actions, and responses.

Note Paul's comments to his disciple Timothy, pastor of the church at Ephesus. The apostle brings to Timothy's attention that the ultimate objective of his ministry is to produce people who love God and one another. Note that his goal is not to reproduce a particular theological system. This love, he reminds Timothy, comes from a heart that is pure, a conscience that is clear, and a life free of hypocrisy (1 Timothy 1:5). Purity, integrity, and authenticity, according to Paul, are the tracks that love runs on.

It makes sense. It doesn't take too much to figure out that impurity precludes integrity and authenticity. Look at it this way: Like falling dominoes, impurity at the level of the heart triggers guilt at the level of the conscience, which results in inauthenticity at the level of life and interpersonal relationships.

To love a neighbor is to respond to that neighbor with authenticity, integrity, and purity. These three qualities play the music of the Gospel. We're talking about introducing your neighbor to a wholesome, fun-loving, authentic, caring, real person . . . you! He isn't interested in meeting the neighborhood conscience or the local fruit inspector. Or the judge and jury.

The fruit of the Spirit, Paul reminds us, is love. Put another way, the evidence of God's presence in our lives is His love at work in and through us. Polluted channels contaminate the flow of God's love. What impurity contaminates, guilt confines and inauthenticity counterfeits. And the world sees masks on people, people playing church, talking a good name, and often worshiping the same gods.

By necessity, lovers are people who regularly invite God

to perform a white-glove inspection of their hearts. It's a daily habit. They have a concern to maintain an inner landscape that pleases God and represents Him in a way consistent with His holy nature. A well-informed conscience is one of God's provisions to keep them building momentum in the right direction. As they respond appropriately to that flashing light on their spiritual dashboard, they grow in integrity and authenticity. Need I say that consistent spiritual disciplines enhance our ability as ambassadors of the King?

Love is light "with skin on." It's tough love. It often means serving without remuneration, suffering without retaliation. Love takes time, energy, and money!

In a most fundamental way, loving a neighbor expresses itself through at least one of three different phases of persuasion. Most of us are gifted in presenting the Good News through at least one of these three windows of opportunity:

> Phase one involves CULTIVATION, which is an appeal to the heart through the building of a relationship.
> Phase two involves SOWING, which is an appeal to the mind through the communication of revelation.
> Phase three involves REAPING, which is an appeal to the will in anticipation of a response.

I guess we could say that evangelism is a three-dimensional process.

A radiant Christian friend works with Muslim and Hindu university students and is seeing many of them discover Christ as their Savior. His success is no surprise. He and his wife have thirty to fifty of them over for dinner each Sunday. (Could it be that the way to a man's heart is through his stomach?)

His own explanation is that he "introduces them to

Christ, but they don't know whom they've met." I like that. They are captured by the purity, the integrity, the authenticity they see and experience, but they have no explanation for it. Intrigued, they want an answer.

"I just keep loving them," he explains, "until they ask me why."

Because his answer has already been sandwiched between the bookends of love and service, his friends do not find Christ offensive. They've heard the music of the Gospel, and they're ready for the words.

Cultivation for this couple begins in the kitchen. An open home, gracious hospitality, and tasty food seasoned with loving service capture the attention of these dear international students and prepare the way for the sowing and reaping phases of evangelism. These phases often involve multiple influences over an extended period of time.

Leveraging people toward the foot of the cross is usually a team effort. Evangelism as a joint venture is an ancient idea. In John 4, our Lord told His disciples He was sending them out to reap what they hadn't sown. Others, he said, had done the hard labor. Please note that reaping is not the hard labor. Any farmer knows that!

Feeding dinner to several dozen hungry collegians each week is hard labor. It's tough love, love that has moved beyond sentiment to service and sacrifice. It's also a love that touches people at a deep level. As such, careful cultivation can eliminate many caricatures that exist in the minds of the lost. Those who cultivate demonstrate, while those who sow explain, and those who reap call to commitment. A "demonstrator" is designed to provide reason for purchasing a particular product. As such, we are "divine demonstrators."

Aren't we to be ready to give an answer "to everyone who asks us the reason for the hope that is within us . . ."? (*See* 1 Peter 3:15.) Why would anyone ask?

> Because they have observed a believer facing the pain and difficulties of life with an unusual hope that defies explanation.
>
> Because someone has enough authenticity that they don't sugarcoat their life and experience and talk a game they're not living.
>
> Because someone dares to defy conventional wisdom.
>
> Because someone has a world view which infuses hope despite the morning headlines.

Maybe the cook's strategy is what Paul had in mind when he wrote, "I have made myself every man's servant, to win over as many as possible" (1 Corinthians 9:19 NEB). No serving, no winning. And here's the principle: When you deal in basic needs, you're always needed. Certainly, part of loving an individual is to meet that person's needs.

We all have physical, emotional, mental, social, and spiritual needs. One of the goals of the effective evangelist is to find that point in a friend's life in which the Gospel becomes Good News and then share it as Good News. Sometimes it is necessary to begin with their felt need (finances, broken relationships, loneliness, etc.) and move to their real need, which is to know Christ.

For the starving, Good News may be a meal served in the name of Christ. For the insecure, the Good News is security in Christ. Those plagued with guilt may find peace through the cross of Christ. Those abandoned and alone often find Christ as their faithful Friend. Even repairing a neighbor's garbage disposal may be used by God to create an interest in the Gospel. All this presupposes, of course, that Christians have non-Christian friends!

To love your neighbor is to serve your neighbor. In so doing we become divine instruments that "play the music" of the Gospel. So how do we play the music?

Playing the Music

First, adopt a servant's attitude. Perspective is everything! True servants don't look down on the unsaved to save them. They look up to them to serve them. Napoleon said, "A man becomes the man of his uniform." Jesus girded Himself with a towel and invites us to also become towel-wearers and basin-bearers. He calls us to a whole new identity.

Unfortunately, sin has blown all our circuit breakers. We are not servants by nature. Furthermore, our culture certainly doesn't put a premium on servanthood. Paul himself had to "make himself a servant." It's a tough choice. Service would be great if it just didn't involve people. Our protective self resists the humility required to use our time, energy, and resources to benefit others.

Second, let them serve you. This advice goes against contemporary wisdom, which suggests that to be a Christian witness we should be paragons of virtue and adequacy. Godly, yes. However, most of us are not perfect partners, parents, or people, for that matter. Scripture encourages us to let our progress, not our perfection, be made known to all men. People want hope, not hype.

We undoubtedly would agree that power is unleashed when needs are met. Something happens when love is more than rhetoric. Bonds are forged and relationships are reinforced as resources are shared. Consequently, the flow of love and concern should not be a one-way street. That pattern makes the recipient feel like a project rather than a person of value and worth.

Christ's ministry to the woman at the well illustrates the fact that often the greatest gift we can share is the gift of our need. Jesus could have snapped His fingers and had an ice-cold Pepsi. Instead, He shared the gift of His need with that lonely, searching woman. Thus affirmed, she quenched His thirst and responded to His offer of living water.

If they offer to bring over a meal, accept their offer. They'd be delighted to pick up something for you at the pharmacy, or drop your kid off at the tennis court. They'd be happy to share their wisdom and experience, if they were asked. A genuine friendship is by nature reciprocal. It's also a victory!

Sometimes the Lord chooses to act in a rather dramatic manner to get our attitudes properly focused. When the Lord sent out the seventy, He insisted that they leave behind their money, food, and extra clothing. They didn't have any baggage to check! Why? They were to be dependent upon the people to whom they ministered. In this important way, Jesus encouraged an attitude of humility, appreciation, and service. Supplied with food, clothing, and shelter, they reciprocated by introducing their hosts to the claims of Christ.

So, when appropriate, let them pick up the tab, call the taxi, host the Christmas party, or fix your garbage disposal.

Third, do an inventory of your gifts and abilities. Evangelism is gift-driven. Every good and perfect gift, Scripture reminds us, is heavenly in its origin. The skilled craftsmen who built the tabernacle were gifted by God for their task, as are evangelists and teachers. Mechanical, electrical, and culinary abilities are gifts that produce spiritual results when brought under Christ's lordship. These gifts are tools. Empowered by God, they uproot soul thistles and thorns. Properly utilized, these divine power tools can cultivate the most hardened soil.

Soul culture is hard work, especially with adults. Their minds are often like bank vault doors. Many have heard the Gospel. Some have "prayed the prayer." Most have stories that will make you weep. Usually they are worshiping the gods of materialism, leisure, and power. Often they are quite content with their present station in life. Underneath it all, however, they have needs. In the name of Christ, we can meet some of them.

If you can fix a car or bake a cherry pie, God can use these skills to "play the music" of the Gospel. I've seen neighbors influenced for Christ by helping them build decks, put in sprinkler systems, or wax their cars. Using such abilities to serve others creates powerful spiritual leverage.

Fourth, view the non-Christian as a victim of the enemy rather than the enemy. His eyes are blinded (2 Corinthians 4:4), and, because of that, the things of God "are foolishness to him" (1 Corinthians 2:14). We should not expect regenerate behavior from unregenerate people. Unfortunately, we sometimes want to get them simonized and Sanforized before they're saved. The "them versus us" attitude has placed a wall between believer and unbeliever that often hinders and distorts the Gospel.

Separated? Yes! But the primary thrust of biblical separation is separation unto God. We are to be both light and salt. The goal is to lose neither our visibility nor our flavor. Certainly separation is not isolation! Our mission is to bring holiness to the hedges, infested though they may be.

Fifth, minister as a joint-venture partner with God. Paul said, "I have planted, Apollos watered; but God gave the increase" (1 Corinthians 3:6 KJV). Exactly! The very love with which you love your neighbor is a gift from God. His Spirit convicts of sin, righteousness, and judgment. We're co-laborers with Him.

A young father is a believer today because he yelled out at a football game, "God, if you'll let my kid score a touchdown, I'll be in church next Sunday." God heard that prayer. On the very next play, the man's son ran sixty yards for a touchdown—the first touchdown, incidentally, his team had scored in six games. The next Sunday, the father went to the church of the pastor who was sitting next to him in the stands. That pastor had purposely positioned himself in that web of relationships and was waiting for "God to give the increase."

God called the play, opened up the hole in the line, and let the right kid score the touchdown. It was no accident the boy's father was sitting next to a pastor who had befriended him. God works in and through us and our circumstances.

Sixth, as you cultivate a friendship, expect God to "stir up the nest." The vast majority of solid commitments to Christ grow out of times of crisis and uncertainty. Fair-weather decisions are rarely lasting. Sometimes God lets people play out their options. Some are ready to listen when they reach the top of the ladder and discover it's leaning against the wrong wall. Others reach the top rung and lose a family. Some see their assets disappear, their kingdoms crumble. Many dreams are shattered by illness and death.

Ultimately, the Gospel is the answer for social, emotional, physical, intellectual, and spiritual concerns. Someone has said that "pain plants the flag of truth in a rebel heart." At the very least, pain gives us the opportunity to listen, share, care, and serve.

God used a can of wax and my elbow grease to influence one family for Christ. My friend loved his car but had physical problems that limited his ability to care for it. I discovered that if you take an interest in what interests another, a bond is formed. The decision to wax his car has had eternal consequences.

A friend of mine reached an elderly neighbor by mowing his lawn on a regular basis. He met a physical need, the grass needed regular attention, and God used his service to meet his friend's need for Christ.

Seventh, "show them what a friend they have in you." For most of them, God is a theological abstraction somehow absent from their lives. They hear the thunder and see the lightning and "look for someone with skin on."

That's you. Your call, as a member of the second incarnation, is to make visible the invisible God, just as Jesus did.

Allowed to get close to you during the storm, they'll ask you the reason for the hope that's in you. Play the music, create a desire for the words! Go with the heart of a servant to meet needs and leverage them toward the foot of the cross.

Eighth, ask God to send you your personal sheet from heaven. Remember, the greatest barriers to evangelism are cultural, not theological. Peter had a divine object lesson designed to help him wrestle with the cultural differences between Jews and Gentiles (Acts 10). Three times he had a vision of a sheet from heaven filled with culturally unacceptable items. He strongly resisted the admonition to "take and eat." No way was Peter going to compromise. Awakened from the vision, he met Cornelius' servants at his door. Gentiles, no less. He invited them in, fed them, and put them up for the night. Cultural barriers went down in every direction. And he took flak from the religious community.

Christians often have a difficult time bridging back into a non-Christian culture because of the cultural expectations of their own Christian communities. They literally become prisoners of these expectations. Some fellowships outwardly preach against any relationship with nonbelievers. "What fellowship," they remind us, "does light have with darkness?" None. Fellowship is based on sharing the nature of God together. Only believers have become "partakers of the divine nature." Friendship, however, is based on sharing the image of God. The entire human race was created in the image and likeness of God. That image, though fallen, we share with fellow human beings.

Ninth, identify points of commonality. Surely there are interests you share. These become touch points, intersections that provide the context for developing a redemptive relationship. To reach a tennis player, become a tennis player. Fishing with a friend alongside a rushing stream is probably a better environment for sharing than a crowded restaurant.

Tenth, commit yourself to regular, specific prayer. Ultimately, we're involved in spiritual warfare. By faith we present our neighbors and friends to Christ. We pray for them daily, and we expect God to open doors and provide opportunities to serve and be served. Praise unleashes the power of God. Things begin to change when the mood of our prayers shifts from petition to praise. We need to pray expectantly.

Eleventh, be prepared to share the words of the Gospel. You may be gifted as a cultivator. My experience has been, however, that many who would never visualize themselves actually sharing the words of the Gospel do indeed lead their friends to Christ. It's a great joy to be present when the new birth takes place. It's a wonderful thing to be a spiritual parent.

Finally, remember . . . love never fails.

Discussion Questions

1. Define *authenticity*, *integrity*, and *purity*. Why does Aldrich single out these three qualities as those that "play the music of the Gospel"?

2. Why shouldn't you be the neighborhood conscience, i.e., pointing out the flaws you see in your neighbors? Or do you disagree with Aldrich? Does this mean that you must be willing to compromise truth?

3. How do you define love? How does Aldrich? How

does the Bible? *See* John 3:16; 1 John 3:16, 4:7–10. How do you reconcile these various definitions?

4. While "evangelizing" essentially means "speaking the Gospel" to the unbeliever, why must we usually do some cultivation before we speak the Gospel?

5. Have you or your church thought of "making disciples" as only one or two of the following: cultivation, sowing, reaping? Which have you included and which have you omitted in your practice of reaching people with the Gospel?

6. What must be our motive for serving? How is Jesus the world's best model of servanthood? *See* Matthew 20:28; Philippians 2:5–8. What examples of servanthood do you see around you? How does our culture run counter to that model, and in what ways does that subtly affect us?

7. Are you selling out on the Gospel if you begin with felt needs? Why or why not? Can you think of a biblical example of beginning with felt needs? *See* Acts 16:27–31.

8. Discuss the wisdom of "let[ting] them serve you."

9. Whose car needs waxing or lawn needs mowing in your neighborhood?

10. How often do you pray for your non-Christian friends? What effect might such prayer have upon both you and them?

5
The Art of Asking Questions

Joel D. Heck

The first sin was set up with a question ("Did God really say . . ." Genesis 3:1), and the first witness attempt was begun with a question ("Where are you?" Genesis 3:9). Ever since that time, good witnesses have learned to apply the art of asking questions. Jim Petersen says, "Any subject, if explored far enough, will lead us into a discussion of the good news."[1] The ability to ask appropriate questions enables any subject to lead to a discussion of the Good News. As a matter of fact, one of the most difficult problems Christian witnesses face is how to get from a discussion of the weather, politics, sports, or current events to a conversation about spiritual matters. The art of asking questions is one of the most effective ways.

Perhaps because the message is the most important part of witnessing, Christians have given too little thought to preparing others to hear the message. If this is true, then emphasis upon listening over the past couple of decades is especially helpful. Good communicators know how to prepare others to hear their message! They are concerned with developing skills in the areas of empathy, listening, and, as we will discuss in this chapter, the art of asking questions.

The Book of Genesis is not the only place in Scripture where a witness began with a question. Philip asked the Ethiopian eunuch, "Do you understand what you are reading?" (Acts 8:30). Peter began a sermon with two questions: "Men of Israel, why does this surprise you? Why do you stare at us as if by our own power or godliness we had made this man walk?" (Acts 3:12). Jesus asked His disciples, "What were you arguing about on the road?" (Mark 9:33). He asked the Pharisees, "What do you think about the Christ? Whose son is he?" (Matthew 22:42). He asked the rich young man, "Why do you call me good?" (Mark 10:18). As a matter of fact, Jesus asked 153 questions of many different people in the Gospel accounts, many of them as an introduction to teaching/witnessing situations!

However, it is not only in Scripture that people recognized the importance of asking questions. A brief survey of some current evangelism literature will reveal the same principle.

Current Evangelism Literature

In his Gospel presentation, D. James Kennedy has popularized the use of two key questions: "Have you come to a place in your spiritual life where you know for certain that if you were to die today you would go to heaven?" and "Suppose that you were to die today and stand before God and he were to say to you, 'Why should I let you into my heaven?' What would you say?"[2] These two questions give clues about the beliefs that are held by the person being visited, and they enable the evangelist to know better how to proceed.

However, not only does Kennedy emphasize these two questions but he also encourages the use of other questions during the introduction to the Gospel presentation, particularly when "their secular life," "their church background," and "our church" are the subjects being discussed. For example, the presenter asks questions about a painting in the living room, the previous home of the person being visited, how the person likes the current city of residence, and the church background of the individual.[3]

Every visitation evangelism approach that shows similarity to Kennedy's approach uses some type of questioning, similar to or identical to the approach Kennedy first formulated. For example, Stephen Biegel, author of *Speaking of Salvation,* includes in the introduction of his outline not only questions about everyday life and church background but also two questions that serve as steppingstones to the message: "May we share with you what the Bible says about eternal life?" and "Why should God let you into His heaven?"[4]

Every community canvass, whether it attempts to present a witness to the Gospel, attempts to discover needs about the community, or seeks to learn community opinion about some issue, asks questions of the people the canvassers contact. Canvassers ask about church affiliation or church background, opinion on various spiritual issues, name, address, interest in another visit, etc. "Are you a member of a local church?" "How often do you attend?" "What led you to drop out?" "What would influence you to come back?" "In your opinion, what ought the Christian church to stand for?" "What do you feel is one of the greatest needs of this area?" "What advice would you give a new church that really wants to help people?"

Most evangelistic home Bible study approaches use the inductive method, drawing participants into the discussion by the use of questions. Ada Lum writes to leaders about the Bible study itself, "Be ready with questions that will stimulate discussion and not simply require one-word answers."[5] Marilyn Kunz and Catherine Schell quote a noted educator who says, "All our knowledge results from questions; question asking is our most important intellectual tool." They continue, "Neighborhood Bible study guides contain many questions to stimulate you to think, and to make fresh discoveries in the Bible."[6] For example, a sample study on Mark 2:1–12 includes these questions: "What indications of Jesus' popularity are there at this time?" "What does Jesus expect to prove to the scribes by healing the paralytic?" "How does the paralytic express his faith?" "What are the reactions to his healing?"[7] Martha Reapsome writes that the key consists not in "telling them the right things, but in asking them the right questions."[8] Albert Wollen likewise states, "As the leader is preparing, he should jot down several questions that could be used to stimulate discussion."[9]

Rebecca Pippert offers three models for moving conversations from ordinary topics to spiritual ones. In Model A, "Investigate, Stimulate, Relate," the investigate phase involves a lot of questioning and a lot of listening. In Model B, "Concentric Circles," borrowed from Donald C. Smith, a former Inter-Varsity staff member in Michigan, she speaks of peeling off the layers of a conversation by going deeper and deeper into a discussion. The conversation begins with general-interest questions and finally asks theological questions. Model C, "Relationships,

Beliefs, Epistemology," was originated by Mark Petterson and published by InterVarsity Press a decade ago.[10] In this model, questions are asked throughout—questions about matters of mutual interest, questions about political or religious beliefs, and questions about why the other person thinks this way.[11] "We must learn to ask questions, draw people out," she writes. "We need to learn how to be listeners first and proclaimers second."[12]

In a recent book on the basics of Christian witnessing, Erwin J. Kolb commends the Q-L-T method. Q-L-T stands for "Question-Listen-Tell,"[13] and Kolb offers quite a number of examples where patient questions and careful listening have provided opportunities to witness. *Ask* lots of questions, *listen* to the answers you receive, and then prepare to *tell* the story of Jesus, he writes. For example, he tells about a conversation with his barber following a snowstorm. They discussed losing business because of the weather, and the barber explained how the snow affected his business. Then Kolb commented, "That's the way it is in church, too, at least at our church." Then a little later he asked, "Is it like that at your church?"[14] That question led to a personal witness about his faith in Christ.

I had a similar experience with a barber. I went to get my hair cut and commented, "I'm going to attend a Christian conference, and I want to look presentable. By the way, do you have any church affiliation?" That question paved the way for hours of witnessing that have occurred since that time.

Even in occupations outside of Christian ministry, for example, in the worlds of counseling, sales, classroom instruction, consulting, investigative reporting, interior decorating, and a host of others, questions are vital to success. There is probably no occupation that does not, in one way or another, use the art of asking questions. While motives and objectives may differ, the counselor, salesperson, or instructor needs to ask questions in order to be effective.

Advantages to Asking Questions

Why are questions so effective in setting the stage for Christian witnessing? First of all, the asking of questions changes the stereotypical view many non-Christians have of Christians. They think Christians are only interested in talking about what they believe. They often feel that Christians are not interested in listening to what others have to say. They see Christians as narrow-minded, self-righteous people who are only interested in spouting off about the Truth.

Second, it provides the witness with the opportunity to learn about the beliefs, misconceptions, hang-ups, life-style, and personal concerns of the non-Christian, with the result that the witness can better speak to those beliefs and concerns.

Third, by asking questions, you are nudging the door of the life of the non-Christian to see whether that door is closed and locked, shut but slightly ajar, open a crack, or wide open to further conversation.

Fourth, it leaves the non-Christian in control of the conversation. The non-Christian is not threatened by such a conversation, since he can always say, "I don't think I want to answer that question" or "That's none of your business." In practicing the art of asking questions, the Christian is like the television set that can be turned off. The non-Christian is the viewer. If the conversation gets too personal, too threatening, or the individual doesn't yet trust the Christian, he can change channels (change the subject) or turn off the set ("I've really got to get going").

Fifth, it provides the Christian with an excellent position from which to handle hostility. If the non-Christian says, "I can't stand religion, and I don't want you cramming your beliefs down my throat," the Christian can say, "I was only asking. I'm not forcing anything on you. God doesn't operate that way, and I don't either."

In the next several pages, I would like to offer a method for asking questions that can enable you to move from a conversation about current events to a conversation about Jesus Christ.

A Proposed Model

The method involves four stages of asking questions, similar to Pippert's Model B, "Concentric Circles." The four stages are these: general informational questions, purpose questions, initial spiritual questions, and deeper spiritual questions. This is not to suggest that all four stages must occur in any given conversation. It may take months or years to get past the first stage. However, the general thrust of these four stages will prove helpful to most.

General Informational Questions

If two people already know each other, this stage may be skipped. However, it is usually the case that even good friends start a conversation with some kind of chitchat.

Here is where you ask, "Where do you work/live/go to school?" "What do you like to do in your spare time?" "How about those Cardinals/Dodgers/Giants/Celtics?" "What do you think about this weather?" "What do you do for a living?" "How do you like living here?" "How is the family?"

At this stage of the conversation, the importance of listening cannot be emphasized enough. The art of asking questions is not a way to manipulate a conversation. It is a way of showing Christian love, of getting better acquainted, of learning how you can meet needs. During this stage, you will discover information you may use later on in the conversation by listening. During this stage, you earn the right to be heard eventually (if you don't listen to him, why should he listen to you?). During this stage, you establish rapport.

This is the kind of question Jesus asked of the disciples at the Sea of Galilee after the resurrection: "Friends, haven't you any fish?" (John 21:5). It is the kind of question two of John's disciples asked of Jesus: "Where are you staying?" (John 1:38).

Purpose Questions

In many instances, you will move from a topic under discussion in the first stage to a purpose question on the same topic. By this question you intend to discover the basic reason(s) or purpose for an individual's life.

If the discussion is among couples and the topic is children, you might ask, "What do you want most out of life for your children?" If the discussion is among college students and the subject is majors, you might ask, "Why are you majoring in psychology/biology?" If the discussion is jobs, you might ask, "Where do you hope to be ten years from now?" You might say, "When your life is over, what do you most want to be remembered for?" If the discussion is current events, you might ask, "What do you think motivates politicians/civic leaders/educators to do that?" You might even ask what they think about some religious leader who has been in the news recently. That would provide you with a good introduction to spiritual matters.

This is the kind of question Jesus asked of the rich

young man: "Why do you ask me about what is good?" (Matthew 19:17).

Initial Spiritual Questions

This is the transition in the conversation from secular matters to spiritual matters. Up to this point, the discussion has not included God. After this point, it will.

In many instances, you will use the topic under discussion in the second stage as your springboard to a deeper level of questioning. If you want to tie this question to what has preceded, you might ask, "What do you think God thinks about all this?" Or you might ask, "Does religion have anything to say about that?"

In some instances, this will not be necessary. People change the subject all the time, so you could ask somewhat abruptly, "Do you believe God is in control of what happens in our lives/world?" It will not be out of place to ask, "What do you think about the church/organized religion/Christianity?" or "Have you ever read about the out-of-body experiences of people who were clinically dead? What do you make of them? Do you believe in life after death?"

This is the kind of question Jesus asked of the lawyer prior to the story of the Good Samaritan: "What is written in the Law?" (Luke 10:26).

Deeper Spiritual Questions

To ask a deeper spiritual question is not as risky as some might think. If the initial spiritual question has been well received, it will not be difficult to move one step deeper.

After some discussion of that initial spiritual question(s), you can ask, "At what point are you in your spiritual life?" You can ask, "Have you ever thought about life after death?" "Are you confident that you will go to heaven?" "What do you think about Jesus Christ?" "Why do you expect to go to heaven?"

This is the kind of question Jesus asked of Peter: "Do you love me?" (John 21:17).

When the conversation has come this far, the sharing of the Gospel is a natural consequence of what has preceded. If, after answering your deeper spiritual question, the non-Christian does not ask, "Well, what do *you* think about life after death?" then you can ask, "May I tell you what I think?" Then tell the person about Jesus.

It is not the purpose of this chapter to help you know what to say at this point. What you say about Christ is the subject of other chapters, particularly "The Art of Speaking the Gospel." The purpose of this chapter is to help you get to the point of being able to share your faith in Christ.

Have these four levels of asking questions overwhelmed you? Does it seem too complicated? Then simply remember this: Ask questions, then ask some more, and ask some more. While you listen carefully, look for an opening to steer the conversation to spiritual matters. Ask first about secular matters, then about interest in spiritual things, and you will soon be able to ask about the heart of the matter: Jesus Christ.

Discussion Questions

1. Do you agree with Jim Petersen's statement, "Any subject, if explored far enough, will lead us into a discussion of the good news"?

2. Is it easier to ask someone's opinion about spiritual matters than to offer yours? Why or why not?

3. What are the advantages of asking questions first as a

prelude to witnessing? Can you list some advantages besides those listed in the chapter?

4. Is it manipulative to ask questions in the manner set forth in this chapter? Why or why not?

5. Can you think of a setting where questions could very well be manipulative?

6. In which of the four levels of questions do the following fit: "Where are you?" (Genesis 3:9). "What do you think about the Christ? Whose son is he?" (Matthew 22:42). "Do you understand what you are reading?" (Acts 8:30). "What do you want?" (John 1:38). You will want to look at these questions in context.

7. Take a subject such as something from current events and work through the four levels of questions, showing how you might move a conversation on that subject to a discussion of spiritual matters.

8. What other initial spiritual questions could you ask besides the ones suggested in this chapter? What other deeper spiritual questions could you ask?

6
The Art of Speaking the Gospel

Roy J. Fish

On visitation night at First Church, Ralph, Bill, and Jack were going to see their friend Joe, who was not a Christian.

"I'm really excited about sharing the Gospel with Joe," said Jack.

"I am, too," responded Ralph. "I'm a little frightened, but I am determined to tell him the Good News."

"How are you going to approach Joe?" Jack asked Ralph.

"I've been giving it some serious thought," Ralph answered. "I really think I ought to begin by saying, 'Joe, you are not getting any younger.' He needs to realize that we don't have forever to make this crucial decision."

"How about you, Bill? What are you going to say?"

"I really feel impressed to try to wake him up. I'm going to remind him that hell is pretty hot and that he is not too far from the furnace. I've always thought it was very important for people to know the consequences of rejecting Jesus. I'm going to remind him of the certainty of God's judgment."

"What about you, Jack?" the other two asked.

"I'm going to stress the importance of immediate commitment. After all, his time for deciding is running out. He could have a fatal accident driving home from work tomorrow. Jesus could come while he sleeps tonight. His time for deciding really is shorter than it's ever been. I want to stress that."

With that, they got in the car and left for Joe's house to share the Good News with him. But if these are the major emphases of their witness to their friend, which one will really speak the Gospel to Joe?

Everything these men had planned to say to Joe is true. None of us is getting any younger. Rejecting Jesus carries serious consequences. There is an urgency in making the right response to Him. But which one was really planning to share the Gospel? Though all three of them were telling the truth, there wasn't a word of Good News or Gospel in anything they planned to share with their friend.

But these three individuals were right about several things. The Gospel is something that is to be spoken. It takes words to get the message across. But what words in particular? What is the content of that message? What is the Gospel? Before one can speak it, one must know its content.

What Is the Gospel?

The word *gospel* comes to us from the Greek through the Latin. The Greek word for "gospel" is *euangelion.* In Latin it became the word *evangelium.* The Greek prefix *eu* means "good." The Greek word *angelia* means "message." Put together, they mean "good message." Evangelism is glad tidings; it is Good News.

Initially, evangelism, or the *euangelion,* was a pre-Christian word describing a message of good news that came from the battlefield. Usually it was related to a message of victory. The church took the word and filled it with sublime meaning. *Gospel* became the word to describe God's saving acts for man as they were accomplished through Jesus.

The writers of our New Testament were keenly interested in showing how this Gospel relates to needy people. This is one reason the Gospel is described in a number of different ways. The New Testament writers portrayed the Gospel as a multifaceted message that speaks to human beings at the point of their deepest needs.

For instance, the Gospel is referred to as the Gospel of peace (Ephesians 6:15). Think of the number of people you know whose lives are deeply troubled. When a medical doctor asked his patients in California what one thing they wanted out of life more than anything else, 87 percent of them replied "inner peace." How relevant the Gospel becomes in a complex world where stress and pressures abound. It is a Gospel of peace.

The Gospel is called the Gospel of hope (Colossians 1:23). In a large southwestern state, an advertising agency was employed by a Christian group to find out the deepest concerns of people who lived there. Number one on their list was hopelessness. In a world filled with despair, the Gospel projects a living hope.

The Gospel is called the Gospel of life and immortality (2 Timothy 1:10). Even in a crassly materialistic world, our dominant instinct is self-preservation. There is something in the hearts of people everywhere—a feeling of incompleteness if life in this world is all there is. Most people like to think there is something after this world that will be better than life as we know it now. This is one of the reasons for the popular emphasis on the mistaken doctrine of reincarnation. The truth of future immortality is a part of our Gospel.

The Gospel is called the Gospel of reconciliation (Ephesians 2:16). Relationships between individuals, families, and even nations are characterized by walls and barriers. The Gospel of Jesus breaks down barriers and walls. It brings people together.

The Gospel is called the Gospel of salvation (Romans 1:16). This word carries with it the thrust of rescue. People sense a need to be rescued from the kind of life they are experiencing. But salvation also suggests a kind of wholeness or completeness. Fragmented people yearn to be whole. The Gospel of salvation speaks to this need.

The Gospel is called the Gospel of the kingdom (Matthew 24:14). This Gospel elevates people in status. It represents something of a transfer of citizenship from an earthly kingdom to the kingdom of God. Life in this kingdom is life of abounding joy and purpose. This Gospel makes us children of God, heirs of God, and joint heirs of Christ. In this kingdom, we are children of the King.

The Gospel is a word which speaks to people whose lives are sinful and broken. It is aimed at those who live in despair. It is intended for those people who are torn apart and those who live with emptiness on the inside. It is for those who are tired of phony living, those who are looking for the real and meaningful in life.

Why Speak the Gospel?

The Christian faith is a faith of facts. Though becoming a Christian is far more than believing certain facts or mentally assenting to a set of accurate propositions, one must know certain facts before one really becomes a Christian. Facts are most objectively described in words.

The Gospel is intended to be spoken because of the intrinsic power of the message itself. The Gospel message is "the power of God for the salvation of everyone who believes" (Romans 1:16). To those who are perishing, "the message of the cross is foolishness," but "to us who are being saved it is the power of God" (1 Corinthians 1:18). We are to lead people to faith in Jesus, and "faith comes from hearing the message, and the message is heard through the word . . ." (Romans 10:17).

What Does the Gospel Say?

What is the content of this Gospel we are to speak? It is defined succinctly in 1 Corinthians 15:1–4: "Now, brothers, I want to remind you of the gospel . . . that Christ died for our sins according to the Scriptures, that he was buried, that he was raised on the third day according to the Scriptures. . . ."

Jesus said essentially the same thing when He commissioned His followers between the time of His resurrection and His ascension. He said to them, "This is what is written: The Christ will suffer and rise from the dead the third day, and repentance and forgiveness of sins will be preached in his name to all nations, beginning at Jerusalem. You are witnesses of these things" (Luke 24:46–48).

Jesus deals with the basics of the Gospel in this passage. First of all, He grounds His message in the Old Testament Scriptures: "This is what is written." Second, He speaks of His saving acts: "The Christ will suffer and rise from the dead on the third day." Third, He sets forth the conditions or requirements by which one becomes a Christian: "Repentance . . . will be preached." Fourth, He declares the benefits of the message: "Forgiveness of sins will be preached." Fifth, He describes the intended audience: "all nations."

Essentially, the Gospel message states what Jesus, through His dying and being raised from the grave, has done to rescue people from their sins. The message is also an invitation to respond to His offer of forgiveness and new life by believing the promises God has set forth.

Planned Presentations or Pure Spontaneity?

Whether or not one who witnesses should employ a planned approach in sharing the Gospel will always be a matter of lively discussion. Though much can be said for a spontaneous, unstructured presentation, most people who share effectively make use of a planned presentation. The manner in which one gets around to the subject of Jesus in a conversation will always be different, altered by circumstances and conditions. But from my observation, most non-Christians who respond to the Gospel do so when the Gospel is shared with them in a planned or predetermined way. Some people are prone to object, "But this is just too simple." But a presentation that is cumbersome and complex can actually cloud the essential truths of God's Word. There is tremendous power in simplicity.

Once a bridge has been built in conversation to the point that one is talking about spiritual things, we want to tell people that God loves them and wants to forgive them and receive them. This can best be done by pinpointing four basic areas that represent something of a systematic verbalization of the Good News. These can be found in a number of books on personal evangelism or in certain pamphlets or tracts that share the message. These four represent something of a basic outline that can be followed when telling somebody about Jesus: (1) God's offer, (2) man's problem, (3) God's provision, and (4) man's response.

God's Offer

Early in my experience as a witness for Jesus, I shared the message by walking down the familiar Roman Road. Using Romans 3:23, 6:23, 5:8, and 10:13, I would begin by telling people they were sinful, lost, and destined for eternal death. I did this for a number of years, hardly realizing there was a much more palatable way of sharing the message without compromising any of its truth. It was an exciting discovery for me to realize that I could begin a presentation of the message by telling people about God's love and God's offer of abundance and eternal life.

How much better it is to begin presenting the Gospel by saying, "God loves you and offers you something," rather than to say to a person, "You are a sinner and bound for death and hell." If the Gospel is really Good News, we should reflect that Good News at the outset of our explanation.

God's purposes for people touch them both in the world of time and in the world of eternity. Speaking of living in the here and now, Jesus said, "I came that they might have life, and might have it abundantly" (John 10:10 NAS). The word *abundantly* literally means "life that overflows with blessings." It is life of great fulfillment, joy, peace, and purpose. This is a part of the Gospel offer that speaks to people in the world of time.

But God's offer also touches people in the world of eternity. "For God so loved the world that he gave his one and only Son, that whoever believes in him shall not perish but have eternal life" (John 3:16). Everlasting life speaks primarily of the quantitative aspect of the life Jesus offers. It is life as long as God lives in eternity. But "eternal life" also has a qualitative aspect. It is the abundant life offered in this world infinitely multiplied in a world to come. This is Good News: God loves you and offers to you abundant and everlasting life.

Man's Problem

Though the Gospel is Good News, it is best understood and more deeply appreciated when presented against the backdrop of the bad news. As a gold watch or a silver ring shines more brightly against a dark velvet cloth, so the Good News of Jesus is even better news when we look at it in light of the universal problem of sin.

The problem arises from our having been given the privilege of choosing whether we will live as God wants us to live or whether we will live as we want to live, go our own way, and do our own thing.

Inevitably, people have chosen the latter. The Bible says it this way: "We all, like sheep, have gone astray, each of us has turned to his own way" (Isaiah 53:6). The choice to go our own way rather than God's way is described in the Bible in terms of a three-letter word: S-I-N. "All have sinned" (Romans 3:23). This is another way of saying that we all have done wrong in choosing our way instead of God's way. In so doing, we have fallen below God's intended standard for us.

The problem of our failure to live up to God's standard is compounded in that it results in our being separated from Him. In the Book of Isaiah, we read, "Your iniquities have separated you from your God" (Isaiah 59:2). The New Testament states this truth succinctly in Romans 6:23: "For the wages of sin is death." It does not speak of cessation or termination but rather of separation and alienation. We are cut off from God, and because of our sin we are missing the kind of life He has designed for us. This experience is described in the New Testament in terms of death.

At this point in sharing the Gospel, it is extremely helpful to illustrate the fact of separation by drawing a diagram. The research of psychologists has shown that generally, people make decisions based on their five senses, and of the five senses, sight is the most important. Some years ago, a prominent book suggested that 87 percent of the decision-making process is based upon the sense of sight. If we draw an illustration, we could be influencing as much as 87 percent of someone's decision-making process. It is Stevens' Law of selling: "Never tell someone what you can show them." The "Bridge Illustration," popularized by the Navigators, or the parallel lines of the "Four Spiritual Laws" or "Steps to Peace With God" are very helpful in graphically illustrating the nature of the problem of sin and separation.

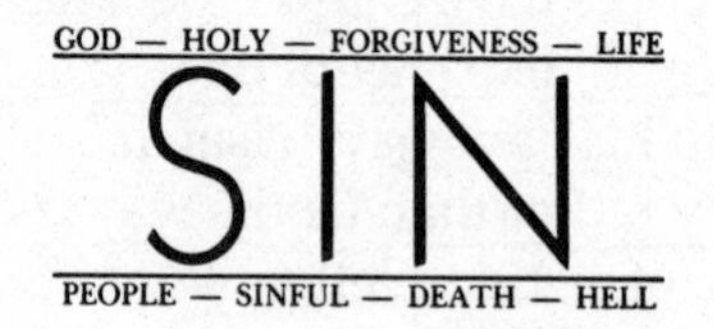

God's Provision

The heart of the Gospel is the fact that God has made provision for our problem of wrongdoing and the alienation it has caused. Essentially, this is the story of Jesus, who He was, and what He did on our behalf. Real Christian witnessing focuses on Jesus. Remember that our witness is not focused toward a plan but a person. Sinful people separated from God desperately need to find a way to Him. There is a way, but only *one* way. The Bible is extremely narrow at this point. Jesus said, "I am the way and the truth and the life. No one comes to the Father except through me" (John 14:6).

Because many people do not realize that the Carpenter of Galilee, Jesus of Nazareth, was God in human flesh, this extremely important fact needs to be brought to their attention. He who existed as God "made himself nothing, taking the very nature of a servant, being made in human likeness" (Philippians 2:7). As God the Son, in a body like ours, He walked on this earth. The Scripture sums up His life this way: "He went around doing good" (Acts 10:38), and in His doing of good, He was totally without sin. The Bible says He "committed no sin, and no deceit was found in his mouth" (1 Peter 2:22). As the sinless Son of God in human flesh, He voluntarily took on Himself our sins and wrongs and died for them on a cross. He became our substitute in suffering for our sins and made a way whereby we could come to God and experience the life He offers (1 Peter 3:18). To help this truth into one's mind, it is useful to go through the eye gate again. A cross should be drawn between the two lines on our diagram, illustrating the fact that through His death, Jesus has bridged the chasm of separation of man from God.

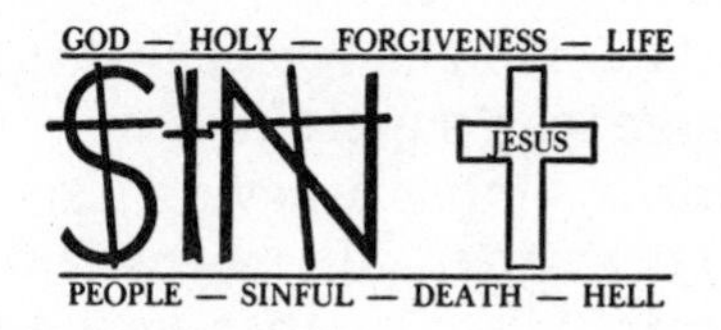

Man's Response

In the five commissions given by Jesus in the four Gospels and the Book of Acts, He set forth two conditions by which people receive the life and forgiveness He offers. Close analysis suggests that these two are so vitally related they are like two sides of the same coin. In Luke, Jesus said that repentance was to be preached among all nations. In Mark, He said that he who believes and is baptized shall be saved. The two conditions are repentance and faith. Paul confirmed this fact for us when he summed up his message: "I have declared to both Jews and Greeks that they must turn to God in repentance and have faith in our Lord Jesus" (Acts 20:21). This is a beautiful summary of the conditions set forth by God by which man comes into a right relationship with Him.

The word *repent* or *repentance* literally means to experience a change of mind. Repentance is a change of thinking that leads to a change of direction in one's life. The essence of sin is our going our own way rather than God's way. It is the refusal to permit God the right to be God in one's life. The essence of repentance is a decision to change and begin to live God's way rather than our way. This can be adequately illustrated by the military command, "To the rear, march!" When a marching column of troops hears this command, the soldiers turn 180 degrees and begin to go the other way.

Repentance is one side of the coin. The other side of the coin is faith.

Faith or belief, as a condition for experiencing God's forgiveness and receiving new life, always means personal trust. It is far more than merely believing facts about Jesus. Intellectual faith or simply believing a set of propositions about Jesus is not saving faith. Saving faith is dependence upon or faith in or toward another person to do something for you. The object of saving faith is Jesus. The objective for which we trust Him is to take our sins and wrongs away, to give us abundant and eternal life, and in doing all of this, to make us right with God. Saving faith might be expressed by inviting Christ into one's heart (Revelation 3:20), receiving Him as Savior and Lord (John 1:12), or simply calling on Him out of a sense of need (Romans 10:13).

The Power of Testimony

What this chapter has dealt with to this point is the Gospel according to Matthew, Mark, Luke, John, Peter, Paul, and others. There is another gospel of which mention should be made. It is the gospel of one's own personal testimony, the good news of what Jesus has done in your life.

Scripture abounds with incidents of people who shared the good news of their own discovery of Jesus. When Andrew had come to know Jesus as the Messiah, "the first thing Andrew did was to find his brother Simon and tell him, 'We have found the Messiah' " (John 1:41). When Philip began to follow Jesus, he found Nathanael and said to him, "We have found the one Moses wrote about in the Law, and about whom the prophets also wrote—Jesus of Nazareth, the son of Joseph" (John 1:45). When the frequently married woman at the well in Samaria believed on Jesus, she went into the city and exclaimed, "Come, see a man who told me everything I ever did. Could this be the Christ?" (John 4:29).

This kind of witness, sharing your experience with Jesus, is actually encouraged by Him. When the man of Gadara had the legion of demons cast out of him, he was so thrilled to be in Jesus' presence that he wanted to stay with Him. Jesus said to him, however, "Go home to your family and tell them how much the Lord has done for you, and how he has had mercy on you" (Mark 5:19). The next verse says, "So the man went away and began to tell in the Decapolis how much Jesus had done for him. And all the people were amazed" (Mark 5:20).

One's own testimony should never be regarded as the basic message. Our primary witness is still a witness to what Jesus has done for us and for all people in dying on a cross. But personal testimony can powerfully attract people to hear and appreciate a more extended presentation of the Gospel.

Many feel that the following outline will get the message of your testimony across effectively: (1) what your life and attitudes were like before you trusted in Jesus; (2) how you came to realize that you needed Jesus; (3) how you personally came to know Jesus as your Savior; and (4) what knowing Jesus as your Savior means to you in your day-by-day life.

Needless to say, if one came to Christ fairly early in life, one might not remember much about the first point in the outline. If that is the case, it would be helpful to share something about the home life in which one was brought up and something about people who were an influence. If one grew up in a Christian home, one should explain that there has hardly been a time in life when some idea of Jesus and the Christian faith was not accepted.

It's very helpful if one commits a brief testimony to memory. To facilitate this, write out your testimony, employing the suggested outline. In so doing, phrases should be brief and simple. Commit it to memory so that you can share it in about a minute and a half. The words employed should be carefully chosen, for many times we are describing an experience with Christ to someone who does not understand religious jargon at all. (The next chapter will explain the importance of your choice of words in more detail.)

When I was a student on a state university campus, I had a great desire to share my faith with others. I knew very little about it and was praying for wisdom when God seemed to say, "You don't know much theology and you don't know much about witnessing, but you do know that I have changed your life. If you want to make an impact on your campus, simply share with others what I have done for you. Let that be your witness for a while."

I had never thought of this before. It was tremendously exciting to think that I had gotten this impression from God, but I wanted to be sure. Perhaps in my immaturity, I prayed what might be looked on as a presumptuous kind of prayer. I said, "God, if you want me to share with others what You've done for me, confirm this by saving the first person with whom I share my testimony."

With that, I left my room, walked down to the dormitory

post office, and there I spotted my man. His name was Bob C. I walked up to Bob and said, "Bob, not long ago I made the most exciting discovery I've ever made. I came to know Jesus Christ in a personal way. I've accepted Him as my Savior, and He's given me wonderful peace in my heart and new purpose for living. I know that someday He will take me to heaven. This is the best thing that's ever happened to me, and I wanted to tell you this because I know He would like to do the same thing for you." This really caught him off guard. He didn't say a word. He just did a quick about-face and ran up the stairs in record time. I thought, *Well, I guess I just missed what God was saying. This must not be the way He'd have me share after all.*

It was necessary for me to leave the campus for three days. I didn't return until Sunday afternoon. One of the first people I saw after I got back was a Christian friend who had been in church that Sunday morning. I asked him, "How were services today? I couldn't be there and I haven't talked to anybody who was." He answered me with real excitement. "We had a wonderful service, and during the invitation Bob C. came forward to accept Jesus as his Savior and Lord." For the first time in my life I realized that God could use the testimony of the gospel according to me. Bob's appetite was whetted by a testimony on Thursday, and he was saved in a service on Sunday.

This chapter began with a study of the Greek word *euangelion*, or "gospel." One form of this word is used in Acts 8:4: "Those who had been scattered *preached the word* wherever they went" (italics added). Judging by the record in Acts, there can be little doubt that they had learned well the art of speaking the Gospel.

If it can be said of us that we, like them, go everywhere, winsomely, boldly, tactfully speaking the Word, perhaps it will also be said of us as it was of them, "These men who have caused trouble all over the world have now come here" (Acts 17:6).

Discussion Questions

1. What is the root meaning of the word *gospel?*

2. In its most concise form, what is the Gospel? Is faith a part of the Gospel?

3. What are some of the topics Christians use in witnessing as substitutes for the Gospel itself?

4. How is the Gospel a message of peace, hope, life and immortality, reconciliation, salvation, or the kingdom? For whom do you need to explain the Gospel in terms of one of these images? Think of a specific person.

5. Can you think of other ways to express the same message in different words?

6. Explain the value of a planned presentation. Has a plan helped you? Under what circumstances might "pure spontaneity" be effective?

7. How would you respond to the charge that Christianity is a narrow religion, intolerant of other beliefs? How does John 14:6 relate to this issue?

8. Can you give your testimony? Would you be willing to give it to the group right now? If you are unable to give a testimony, write one out during the next week and share it with someone.

9. How can a testimony be misused? That is, who can become the focus of a testimony rather than Christ? Can you give any biblical examples of testimonies?

7
The Art of Using Appropriate Vocabulary

Dick Innes

On one occasion, soon after I arrived in the United States from overseas, I recall entering an old-fashioned elevator in Chicago and announcing to the operator, "Eighth floor, please!"

"What floor?" he queried.

"Eight!" I repeated in my finest Australian English.

"Ite!" he exclaimed. "What's ite?"

I made several more futile attempts to communicate which floor I wanted. Finally, in frustration, I blurted out, "The one after seven, please!"

"Oooh," he said, "you want aaate!"

"Right!" I replied with much relief.

At best, communication can be very difficult—at worst, disastrous. Just because I have spoken doesn't mean I have communicated. To communicate effectively means that the listener needs to hear and understand my message as closely as possible to what I meant it to be. We know that effective communication is much more than words, but words are central to any message we desire to proclaim. Used poorly, words can confuse and mislead. Used wisely and powerfully, they can move much more than mountains. They can move individuals and nations.

The Power of Words

Imagine, if you can, living in a world without language, speech, or words. What would such a world be like?

Words are one of God's richest gifts to us. They are a mark of higher intelligence. They set us apart from the animal world. Animals can communicate with one another through sound, sight, smell, and touch (as can we), but animals can't communicate to each other through words.

As Peter Cotterell of London says, "Human speech is really a remarkable thing. Although porpoises make all kinds of interesting noises and although dogs may collect a vocabulary of maybe twenty or more human words, there is absolutely nothing in the animal world remotely like the complex phenomenon of human speech."[1]

Words are the vehicle we use to convey thoughts and ideas from one mind to another. We think in words—at the rate of fourteen hundred per minute! We teach with and learn through words. We communicate our noblest thoughts, our most heroic aspirations, and the deepest longings of our hearts through words.

With words we can make some people laugh, others cry. We can inspire, motivate, and encourage some; others we can aggravate, discourage, or make feel guilty and ashamed. We can move some to love us, others to hate us. With words we can persuade some to perform noble deeds of kindness, others, if we are so inclined, to deeds of evil. Such is the power of words.

Men and women who have moved their world are those who have mastered the use of words—spoken or written, often both.

Napoleon once said, "There are only two powers in the world—the sword and the pen; and, in the end, the former is always conquered by the latter." Benjamin Franklin, referring to movable type, once said, "Give me twenty-six lead soldiers, and I'll conquer the world."

Recall the words of Winston Churchill during World War II when England was on the brink of collapse. Invasion by Germany seemed imminent. Forty-seven of England's warships had been sunk in the operations off Norway after Dunkirk. The Royal Air Force had lost 40 percent of its bomber strength. Britain was threatened by famine. Her armies were without arms or equipment. When all seemed lost, Churchill went on the radio and inspired the British people with these immortal words: "We shall defend our island whatever the cost may be; we shall fight on the beaches; we shall fight in the fields; we shall fight in the streets; we shall fight in the hills. We shall never surrender. . . ." Churchill appealed to the American people: "Give us the tools and we'll finish the job!" The rest of the story is history.

Think, too, of the power of words commanded by men like Abraham Lincoln and Martin Luther King. They changed their worlds through their words. Remember Hitler, too, who, through his mastery of words, captured the leadership of Germany and plunged much of the world into tragic chaos.

The late dictator of Romania was so afraid of the power of the written word that he forbade any literature to be published that was not under his direct control. People even had to have a license to own a typewriter!

The Chinese feel so strongly about the power of the written word that they have a saying, "The printed page will conquer."

God Himself used words to communicate His truth to mankind. We are to do the same. As the Bible says, "For since in the wisdom of God the world through its wisdom did not know him, God was pleased through the foolishness of what was preached to save those who believe" (1 Corinthians 1:21). And again, "How, then, can they call on the one they have not believed in? And how can they believe in the one of whom they have not heard? And how can they hear without someone preaching to them? . . . Consequently, faith comes from hearing the message, and the message is heard through the word of Christ" (Romans 10:14, 17).

Whether words are preached, spoken informally, taught, or written, they are essential for communicating the Gospel. However, if our words are heard but not listened to, no communication has taken place. If they are misunderstood or antagonize people, they communicate a negative message and can drive people further from the cause to which we are seeking to draw them.

We have only communicated effectively when the listener has paid attention to our message and understood it as we intended. Peter Cotterell agrees. He says, "Perfect communication takes place when my *conception* matches your *perception*, when I have a message I want to share with you and you get *exactly* that message. Unfortunately, perfect communication is rare."[2] Fortunately, communication doesn't have to be perfect to be effective, but it does need to be as clear as possible.

As communication is much more than words, so Christianity is much more than talking. It is experiencing divine love, divine acceptance, and divine forgiveness and communicating these to every life we touch. It is a profound message that God has entrusted to us. We show our Christianity through our actions and explain it through our words.

In this chapter, we are discussing how to explain the Gospel. If words are the means for doing this, how can we use them for the greatest impact? First we will look at five approaches to avoid and second, five approaches to follow to ensure that our communication of the Gospel is as effective as possible.

Part I

Avoid the Language of Zion

Recently my favorite motivational speaker was in town, so I went to hear him. I have listened to his tapes for hours in my car. What he has had to say has made quite an impact on my life. I decided that I was going to meet him that day. Five minutes before his lecture began, I was standing in the foyer of the auditorium waiting for a friend. Scores of people were coming in when I saw a man I thought looked like the speaker. He walked straight toward where I was standing. Our eyes met. I said, "Excuse me, are you so-and-so?" He said, "Yes." We introduced ourselves, and he said, "Let's grab a quick cup of coffee."

I thanked this man for the impact his ideas had made on my life. As we headed to the auditorium, I said, "You have quoted from the Bible several times in your lectures. Are you a Christian?" He replied, "All depends on what you mean by a Christian."

Now what do I say? I had about one minute left. *Do I ask him if he is saved or born again or some other God-talk stuff?*

I could hardly believe what was happening. I had the

opportunity to witness to one of the nation's leading motivational speakers. How could I communicate to him in one minute?

"What do I mean by being a Christian?" I said. "Well, let me put it this way: I hate churchianity, but I am sold on real Christianity. Christ didn't run around asking people if they wanted religion or if they wanted to be saved. He asked people if they wanted to be healed and made whole. That's what Christianity is all about. It's an exciting message."

Time was up. The man was gone. I felt confident that I had communicated, because in his opening remarks to the audience he talked about the importance of being made whole!

There will be times when it is appropriate to talk to a non-Christian about being born again. However, I would first ask that person if he or she understood the term *born again* and, if not, could I explain it.

As far as we know, there was only one person Christ ever told he needed to be born again, and that was Nicodemus, who was already a devout believer in God and very close to the kingdom.

Had I asked this secular speaker if he were born again (or used some other churchy terminology), and he had no idea what I was talking about, he may very well have dismissed me as another religious weirdo.

Most people who are reading this book are not too likely to use way-out church jargon such as telling their neighbors they need to be washed in the blood of the Lamb. One could readily imagine what images such language would conjure up in the minds of nonbelievers! However, as one who continually writes material to be given to nonchurch people, I find it is an ongoing challenge to avoid using churchy language I have grown up with and take for granted. Words like *salvation, justification, regener-*

ation, righteousness, sanctification, atonement, conversion, evangelism, redemption, and *being lost* have little meaning, if any, to non-Christians. Many of these words can be confusing and a turnoff.

In his article "The Vocabulary of Evangelism," Joel Heck suggests that instead of using the word *justification* we try "made right with God." Instead of *sanctification,* try "living the Christian life." For *regeneration,* use "becoming a Christian," for *righteousness,* substitute "goodness," for *atonement,* try "sacrifice," and so on.[3]

I find, too, that when I write for non-Christian readers, I rarely use the name "Holy Spirit" and never "Holy Ghost." I say "the presence of God." I usually list Scripture references as footnotes—the same as I do with most other references. Little things like "(John 3:16 TLB)" and "(Romans 10:9, 10 NIV)" in the text wouldn't mean a thing to me if I had no biblical knowledge. Furthermore, they clutter the text.

If I talk about sin, which I need to do, I try to explain it. For example, sin is not certain actions that God happens not to like. It is much more than external behavior such as lying, cheating, stealing, and so on. It is anything less than the perfection or maturity God envisioned for us. It is a lack of forgiveness, having impaired relationships, mixed motives, and even following a set of rigid, legalistic rules and feeling self-righteous in doing so. It is being less than whole. It is having damaged emotions and unresolved hurt, fear, anger, guilt, and shame—out of which so many of our negative acts, addictions, broken relationships, and physical diseases come. Sin is totally destructive of human personality. It destroys what God loves: us! Its end result is both physical and spiritual death. This is why God is so opposed to it.

If we don't need to use churchy words, let's not. But when we do, we need to make sure our listeners understand what they mean. Unless you are a lawyer or a legal buff, "legalese," the language lawyers use, can drive you crazy. "Christianese," the language Christians often use, can have the same effect on non-Christians.

Avoid Being Pushy and Insensitive

Some time ago I had an accident at work that put me in the hospital for a week. I shall never forget one of the nurses who attended me. She was a Christian and was trying to convert me to her particular brand of religion. At the time I was in considerable physical pain and was feeling very ill and miserable. This nurse stood at my bedside telling me truths I already knew. She quoted Bible verses to me. She preached at me. She was obnoxious. I wanted her to go away and leave me alone. Had she just held my hand and asked if there was anything she could do to help me feel more comfortable, I would have been much more receptive to what she had to share with me. When I felt better, I might even have asked her about her beliefs. As it was, I rejected her message and didn't want anything to do with her or the product she was pushing.

I'm particularly impressed with the manner in which Jesus ministered to people. He always acted and spoke with authority but was never authoritarian. He never forced His ideas on anyone. He always gave people the freedom to accept or reject Him and His message. For example, consider the rich young man who fell on his knees before Jesus and asked, "Good teacher, what must I do to inherit eternal life?" (Mark 10:17).

Apparently this man was living a very moral and upright life, but he had one major weakness: the love of money. Jesus knew that when He put His finger on this problem, the young man would reject His message, but this didn't affect His love for him.

As the record says,"Jesus looked at him and loved him.

'One thing you lack,' he said. 'Go, sell everything you have and give to the poor, and you will have treasure in heaven. Then come, follow me.'

"At this the man's face fell. He went away sad, because he had great wealth" (Mark 10:21, 11).

Another way we can be insensitive is by trying to push people too quickly into receiving Christ.

Evangelism is a process, not an event. Physical birth is preceded by a nine-month gestation period. Spiritual birth can take years in gestation. In our instant-food, instant-cash, instant-gratification society we want instant maturity, instant healing, and instant evangelism. It rarely works that way. With little, if any, regard to the level of spiritual awareness or Gospel understanding in our non-Christian contacts, some of us were taught a rather aggressive form of evangelism that shares the plan of salvation and invites the "listener" (often a complete stranger) to receive Christ and make a life-changing decision in about ten to fifteen minutes. If we're not careful, this can readily become "wham-bam" evangelism.

True, some people do come to Christ quickly and easily. In such cases, the seed usually has been sown already and the persons responding are ready to be harvested or born. These are the heads we count to prove our method is successful. But who counts the heads of all the stillborn babes and the many we drive away from the kingdom because of our insensitive approach?

There are always exceptions, but ask any group of Christians how many received Christ as Savior the very first time they ever heard anything about the Gospel. It is rare to find even one.

Furthermore, most people strongly resist change, especially when their personal beliefs are being challenged. According to psychologists, people have only a limited "latitude of acceptance." That is, they are only willing to accept change a little bit at a time. Even if we don't use an insensitive manner to seek to persuade people to come to Christ, if we try to move them too far too fast, we run the risk of pushing them into their "latitude of rejection."

As Em Griffin explains, any ideas that don't fit into a person's latitude of acceptance will be seen as "far out" and automatically be rejected. "In fact, they may even trigger a boomerang effect and drive him farther away."[4]

Once the seed of God's Word has been planted in a person's mind (and that can take many attempts), months or even years of cultivation can pass before the fruit is ready to be picked. This is why continual sowing and cultivation are needed.

Echew Obfuscation

I was amused by a cartoon reprinted from *Saturday Review* in Griffin's book.[5] A well-built police officer has dragged in a harmless-looking fellow and is presenting him to the police chief with the following accusation: "He had this dirty bumper sticker on his car. It said ESCHEW OBFUSCATION."

Peter Cotterell gives us a good example of obfuscation—a word that makes my tongue fall over itself when I try to say it! Cotterell tells about a time he was visiting a church in an English industrial city. He said the pastor's "sermon title was: 'The Significance of Some Current Interpretations of the Intertestamental Period of Modern Study.' It was! I heard it! And this was in an area where people make cars for a living."[6]

I think this preacher meant that he was going to talk about what happened during the time between the Old and New Testaments of the Bible! Who knows?

It's a bit like saying, "A disseminator of kernels went forth to implant kernels. As he was dispersing the kernels throughout the area of his tilled fields, some kernels happened to be misdirected and alighted atop the path. . . ."

Perhaps he could have said, "A farmer went out to sow his seed. As he was scattering the seed, some fell along the path. . . ." Jesus did (Matthew 13:3, 4).

One thing is certain: Jesus never used fancy words, religious terminology, obscure words, or any words or phrases that His hearers didn't understand. They didn't always understand or accept His message (because they didn't want to), but He never used words they couldn't understand. Jesus' simplicity was a part of His genius.

Avoid Talking the Party Line

There's a certain party line that many of us evangelicals unfortunately get hooked into. It can include God-talk but can be much more subtle. David Seamands, well-known author, pastor, and seminary lecturer, calls it "Christianizing our complexes."

An inappropriate use of the phrase "Praise the Lord" is a simple example. I remember working on a church building project when one of the men hit his finger with a hammer. It hurt like crazy and all he said was "Praise the Lord!" with a grin on his face. I can't help but wonder what he might have said had he not been surrounded by a group of Christians. Certainly there is a time to say, "Praise the Lord," but there is also a time to yell, "Ahhhhhh!" If I weren't a Christian and somebody hit his finger with a hammer and cried or yelled out his true feelings, I'd be much more inclined to listen to him in other matters than listen to somebody who has a habit of inappropriately expressing religious cliches.

Another party-line phrase is "Are you in the Word?" I've had it said to me when I've been feeling in the pits. It's about the same as asking a man who hasn't eaten for days and is starving, "Are you in the Word, brother?"

When it comes to Christianizing our complexes, I've heard little-known and well-known preachers alike tell me that if I'm having problems I need to be filled with the Holy Spirit, or, as already noted, get into the Word, or even worse, my problems are demons! I was in a meeting once where a popular speaker blamed just about every human problem imaginable on demons. Some may have been, but most were everyday emotional problems. He was even "casting out" the demon of tooth decay. Amazing!

I've also heard evangelists say, "Jesus is the answer to your loneliness" and "If you *give your heart to Jesus* [whatever that means to a non-Christian], you will find the inner peace your heart craves." Well, I came to Jesus forty-five or so years ago, and He never took away my loneliness, and it's taken me years to find inner peace . . . and some days I realize I haven't fully arrived yet.

What these well-meaning evangelists didn't say or explain was that when I received Christ I would find peace with God and He with me (which is of unspeakable value), but it could take years of growth and maturity to make and find peace with myself and other people—which also happens to be the answer to loneliness! If, like me and thousands of others, you came from a dysfunctional family, overcoming loneliness and finding inner peace can be a long, painful struggle.

Furthermore, telling people "Jesus is the answer" or that "God loves you and I love you, too" is not enough. Love without action, without support, and without providing a way to help people face and resolve their private battles is sentimentality, or, as a counselor acquaintance calls it, sloppy agape!

The object of this chapter is not to explain how to find peace and overcome personal problems. The purpose is to recognize and avoid false and meaningless cliches in our witness for Christ. They are like clouds without rain in a dry and thirsty land.

"Therefore each of you must put off falsehood and speak truthfully to his neighbor" (Ephesians 4:25).

Avoid Intellectualizing the Gospel

I once asked the question in an adult Sunday school class, "What is the answer to sex and the single adult?" The class had one answer: "You get married."

"And what if you don't?" I asked. "But you do," they all agreed (everybody in the class that day happened to be married). Well, almost everybody agreed. I didn't, and neither did the teacher. The teacher's answer was profound. He said, "No, the answer to sex and the single adult is total abstinence because if you're not getting any sex, you lose your drive for it!"

I wonder how the millions of singles in this country would feel about these answers. Many of them may not get married for years and many others, never!

Whether the problem is being single or any one of a number of other problems that are plaguing contemporary society (including the church)—alcohol, drugs, incest, adultery, sex, work, food, spending, broken homes, divorce, physical, emotional, and sexual abuse, depression, loneliness, fear, anxiety, homosexuality, abortion, codependency, and so on—we need to do much more than give simplistic answers that require no involvement or commitment. When we fail to face these issues head-on and do something positive to help people overcome their private battles, even though we teach the Scriptures faithfully and share the plan of salvation clearly, we make the Gospel nothing more than an intellectual exercise—a biblical head trip.

Jesus said, "You will know the truth, and the truth will set you free" (John 8:32). To find freedom from bondage, we not only need to know God's truth but we also need to apply it to the truth about ourselves. That's how we personalize the Gospel!

If evangelism is going to be effective in this decade, we must find answers to the problems people are struggling with. The New Age movement is doing this and thriving in the process. It is filling a vacuum that we in the church have helped create because we have intellectualized rather than personalized the Gospel.

Without access to people's personal truth, there is no freedom and no healing. Our responsibility as Christ's witnesses is to apply the truth of God's Word to the truth of people—to exactly where they are! So many of our sicknesses (physical, emotional, and spiritual) are caused by denial. Jesus always personalized His message to get beyond the individual's defenses and denial to the real issue. To the woman at the well, who was shacking up with some fellow, He said, "Go fetch your husband!" To blind Bartimaeus, who had a physical problem, "What do you want?" To the invalid at the pool of Bethesda, He said, "Do you want to be made whole?" We need to do the same.

There we have five ways *not* to communicate the Gospel. Now let's look at five ways to make communicating the Gospel creative, satisfying, and effective.

Part II

Make Communication Two-Way

In the mid-1920s, secular magazine publishers, realizing the importance of getting feedback from their subscribers, began to conduct readership research, or what is known as "subscriber profile analysis." They conducted surveys with their readers to find out what their needs and interests were, to ensure that their magazines were addressing these issues and to see if the material they were writing was being read. Secular publishers and communicators depend very heavily on two-way communication, without which they would go out of business very quickly.

Evangelical publishers began to do this type of research fifty years later. Some still need to, since the same principle applies to communicating the Gospel, whether it is in mass communications or in personal witness.

Jim Engel reminds us that "one point is perfectly clear: People are not robots. They see and hear what they want to see and hear through a complex procedure of information processing. Because they have this God-given ability to ignore us if they choose, it places a demand on the communicator to be audience-oriented."[7]

What Engel and the secular publishers are telling us is this: If people are going to listen to us, we need to ask, not assume, what their interests and needs are, and then address their specific needs. This obviously requires two-way communication.

In the past, most training in evangelism began with a program that was applied to almost everyone without taking into consideration the needs of the listener.

We wouldn't preach the Gospel to starving people overseas before feeding them. The same principle applies at home. If people are going to consider the Gospel, they need to know we are concerned about them as persons. We need to minister to people's needs—not only to earn the right to be heard but also because that's what the Gospel is all about.

We need to be sensitive and tactful, of course, but we find out what people's needs are by asking them and giving them an opportunity to talk. However, people will open up to us only if they sense that we are genuinely interested in them, are safe to talk to, are accepting and nonjudgmental, and won't give them pat or canned answers.

If we don't have an answer to a person's need, let's admit it. For example, last week a distraught mother who has a mentally retarded son was crying as she was sharing with our church care group how much taking care of her son was draining her. She sees no end to her problem and no hope for any kind of healing. Should I have told her that God loves and cares for her and sent her on her way? The fact was, I didn't have an answer and admitted it. All I can do is encourage her to keep coming to our care group, get her feelings out, and share her needs with us so our church can find practical ways to help her and her family.

The Apostle Paul also believed in two-way communication. "Yes," he said, "whatever a person is like, I try to find common ground with him so that he will let me tell him about Christ and let Christ save him. I do this to get the Gospel to them and also for the blessing I myself receive when I see them come to Christ" (1 Corinthians 9:22, 23 TLB).

Scratch 'em Where They Itch

Isn't it amazing? You can call and call your kids on a hot day to come and help you clean up the yard, but somehow they don't seem to hear a word you say. If they do, they're not listening anyhow. Your message bounces right off the tops of their heads. It can be exasperating. But call them from their work to come in out of the heat and have a cold drink and ice cream?

How many times have our wives, husbands, or kids spoken to us, and we were completely oblivious to what they had to say or ask? Why do we hear some messages and not others? What makes the difference?

We are continually bombarded by so many messages

that it is impossible to take them all in, so we filter out most things that don't in some way speak to our felt or perceived needs and interests. The God-given filter we have is called the "reticular activating system." Apparently it is a grouping of nerves shaped like half an apple, located in the middle of the brain. It is as if everybody has their own built-in Apple computers in their heads that process all incoming information. If the information is relevant to our needs, it gets immediate access to our attention. If not, it is filtered out—or we shape the incoming information to fit our particular felt needs.

To illustrate my point, how do you read the following statement? "Loveisnowhere." Did you read it as "love is now here" or as "love is nowhere"? Your answer will depend on your felt need—whether or not you feel loved at this point in time.

Because felt needs affect us so strongly, people are very selective in what messages they will expose themselves to, which ones they will pay attention to, how they perceive and distort messages to match their felt needs and feelings about themselves, and which messages they choose to remember. Communicators explain this principle further as follows:

"*Selective exposure* shows that people will only be open to messages they wish to receive.

"*Selective attention* shows that people hear only what they want to hear.

"*Selective comprehension* or perception shows that people will perceive [and see] things the way they want to see them.

"*Selective distortion* shows how people may change messages to match their self-concept [and how they are feeling at the moment].

"And *selective retention* shows that people remember only what they want to remember.

"Everything else is filtered out."[8]

As Christian communicators, we ignore these principles to our peril. We simply cannot overemphasize the fact that if people are going to listen to the Gospel (or any other message), what we say must speak to the needs our listeners are feeling. We need to minister to *their* needs and not *out of our own!*

Knowing that people's spiritual need is the most important need can tempt us to seek to meet that need first. However, if they don't *feel* that need, that is, are not conscious of it, they won't be interested in what we have to say. Their filters will block it out, and their minds will remain closed to our message.

Felt needs are always at the conscious level of people's minds, while real or spiritual needs are often at the unconscious level. If we address our message to the unconscious need, it is filtered out; if to the conscious need, it is given immediate attention. Felt needs occupy the conscious mind and drive people. However, once a felt need is met, it is no longer a drive and no longer fills a person's mind. This then opens the way for other unmet needs to rise to consciousness, where they become felt needs. This is how felt needs eventually lead to real needs.

When spiritual need is not felt in any way and the mind is closed, the seed of God's Word falls by the wayside. When spiritual need is felt and the mind is open, the seed has a chance of falling on fertile soil.

If you find a need, meet it. If you find a hurt, heal it. In other words, scratch people where they itch. That's what Christianity is all about. It also happens to be the key for opening closed minds and getting our message heard . . . and accepted!

The key to understanding people's felt needs—whether our audience is one person, one hundred, or one thousand—is to ask them. That's the language we need to talk.

Show Me, Don't Tell Me

Let's face it: without emotion, persuasion bores us to tears.

As important as logic is, it doesn't move people to act or make life-changing decisions. People are moved by emotion. They make decisions not only on the basis of what information and facts they have but also with their hearts on the basis of how they feel.

People need facts to know what decision to make but emotion to get them to make the decision. As Em Griffin puts it, "Emotions are what move us—logic tells us which direction to go. Feelings show us our need—rational thoughts suggest solutions to meet that need."[9] In persuasion, both logic and emotion are needed. Even if people are going to listen to us, we need to hook into their feelings. It's not logic but emotion that grabs people's attention and turns them on.

So if emotion is needed for effective communication and witnessing, how can we get people emotionally involved and not get caught up in sticky emotionalism? The answer is to use personal stories (your own and others), parables, and graphic word pictures—what counselors Gary Smalley and John Trent call "emotional word pictures."[10] This is one of the most powerful ways to communicate any message.

Smalley and Trent explain how emotional word pictures were the "primary method that:

- ancient wise men used to penetrate the hearts and minds of men and women;
- Abraham Lincoln and Winston Churchill utilized to inspire their countries in times of great peril;
- Hitler used to capture and twist the soul of a nation;

- top sales managers utilize to train effective employees; and
- comics and cartoonists have mastered to make us laugh while challenging us to think."[11]

Jesus and the writers of the Bible used this method to communicate many of God's truths. Jesus, of course, was the Master Communicator and Storyteller and constantly used word pictures in His many parables to teach people spiritual truths.

When Becky Pippert was an agnostic, she pictured Jesus as being something of a limp-wrist. This is how she describes what changed her opinion of Him:

> One day I looked at the New Testament. Instead of a meek, mild Jesus, I found a man of profound passion. An extraordinary being, flinging furniture down the front steps of the temple, casting out demons, and asking people how they expected to escape the damnation of hell. He said such bland, innocuous things as, "I came to cast fire on the earth." G. K. Chesterton points out that even his literary style reflects his passion. He writes, "The diction used *about* Christ has been, and perhaps wisely, sweet and submissive. But the diction used by Christ is quite curiously gigantesque; it is full of camels leaping through needles and mountains hurled into the sea." Moreover, his style consists of "an almost furious use of the 'a fortiori.' His 'how much more is piled one upon another like castle upon castle in the clouds.' After seeing this shattering personality which fills the gospels, having gotten even a glimpse of him, I could never, never again say with casual indifference, "Oh, how interesting."[12]

True, Jesus was a Man of passion and emotion as well as a Man of extraordinary logic. But He communicated His logic through the use of parables, stories, illustrations, and emotional word pictures.

Speaking to felt needs *grabs* a person's attention. Stories, illustrations, and emotional word pictures *hold* their attention and communicate the message we want them to hear, as Jill Briscoe's chapter on storytelling will demonstrate.

"When it comes down to a contest between a storyteller and a didactic preacher," says Griffin, "the storyteller will carry the day every time." He continues:

> My specific advice for you is to use words that help your listener call up in his mind the same image that you have in yours. Don't just talk about the power of God in the abstract. Who knows what he'll picture if you leave it that vague? Use a specific example as a springboard. Talk about Christ stilling the waves as reported in Mark 4. Get him to visualize the small boat plunging down the backside of a twenty-foot wave. Get him to see the desperation on the disciples' faces as they scream, "Master, don't you care that we're drowning?" Stimulate his other senses as well. Encourage him to hear the roar of a forty-mph gale that snatches away every yell. Get him to feel the numbing ache of muscles straining against the oars—the sting of salt spray in the membrane of the eyes and nose. Then contrast this chaos with the dead calm which followed Jesus' command. If you get the listener to mentally place himself in this situation, he'll gain a new appreciation of Christ's power.[13]

You want me to listen to you? Then tell me a good story. Tell me your story—your experience. It is perhaps the most effective way of witnessing you have. Only if Christianity works for you will you have any chance of convincing me or anybody else that it will work for us. If it does, tell me.

Be Real

On one occasion, I became impatient with two high-pressure salesmen and told them off. Unknown to me, one of the non-Christian women on my staff overheard what I said. That night she went home and said to her husband, who was very antichurch at the time, "You'll never believe my new boss. He's supposed to be a minister of religion and he said such-and-such. He's real!"

Both had been in church as children, but they had long since turned from God and the church. Seeing me as human was the beginning of their turning back to God and the church.

Now, I'm not suggesting that as a way of witnessing we run around telling people off! I *am* suggesting that we be real. People want to see us as human, having the same feelings and problems they struggle with, but they want to see how, with Christ's help, we are coping and are in the process of overcoming. If we come across as "holier than thou," without any problems, people will picture us with our heads in the biblical clouds and will dismiss us as phony.

Another thing that impacted my employee and her husband for Christ was inviting them to a share group where the rest of us were Christians and where we all took down our masks and let one another see the real us—warts and all. Years later, that employee is still working in our organization and plays a vital role in our publishing the Gospel, and her husband directs our Australian ministry! Seeing Christians as real turned them toward Christ.

As already pointed out, our personal story is a powerful way to evangelize. However, people need to see us being realistic about life, and, above all, honest and authentic.

It isn't always so. Griffin says:

> The "testimony" has become a mainstay of Christian persuasion. The typical testimony is told by the

> successful businessman, beauty queen, or sports hero. The story line usually consists of how rotten things were, of becoming a Christian, and of how great things are now. This is devious because it suggests that all these good things will come to the listener if he turns to Jesus. It's similar to the deception of TV commercials which promise sex appeal from a toothpaste, popularity from a mouthwash, or the undying love of your husband if you serve the right brand of coffee.[14]

Christianity is for sinners, not "saints." It is for those who realize that we need a power greater than our own if we are going to make it. It isn't for those who have already arrived. It is for those who are in the process of becoming. It is for people who acknowledge their sinfulness and their need of a Savior. It is communicated most effectively by those who admit this and are real.

"You know what affected me most?" said a young woman whom Rebecca Pippert was seeking to win to Christ.

> All my life I used to think, "How arrogant for someone to call himself a Christian, to think he's that good." But then I got to know you—and Becky, you are far from perfect, yet you call yourself a Christian. So my first shock was to discover you blow it like I do. But the biggest shock was that you admitted it, where I couldn't. Suddenly I saw that being a Christian didn't mean never failing, but admitting when you've failed. I wanted to keep Christ in a box and let you be religious during Bible studies. But the more you let me inside your life, the more impossible it became to keep the lid on Christianity. Even your admission of weakness drove me to him![15]

"To win some we need to be winsome." Being real is one of the most effective ways to do this.

Be Christ

Picture Jesus walking down the hot, dusty streets of Jericho with the crowds pressing in on Him from every side. It seemed the entire town wanted to see this amazing miracle worker. One man in the crowd was Zacchaeus, a despised tax collector for the Romans. He would have been about as popular as a Palestinian collecting taxes from fellow Palestinians for the Israelis—and getting paid for doing it! In other words, people hated his guts.

Determined to see Jesus, and having come in the economy size, Zacchaeus climbed a sycamore tree so he could see above the crowd. Think how he must have felt when Jesus noticed him among the hundreds of people, came over to the tree, and began talking to him. He probably felt excited, anxious, amazed, and afraid all at the same time.

Could you imagine Jesus looking up at Zacchaeus, introducing Himself, and then saying, "May I ask you a personal question? If you should die tonight, do you know where you would go?" I can see Zacchaeus being so shocked that he falls out of his tree and discovers first-hand, alas, too late, where he is going!

No, Jesus, sensitive to the needs of individuals, looked up and said, "Zacchaeus, come down immediately. I must stay at your house today" (Luke 19:5).

Jesus didn't quote any Bible verses or use any kind of religious jargon with Zacchaeus. He didn't even discuss spiritual things—at least not until He ministered to his personal need. Knowing how Zacchaeus was hated and rejected because of his bootlicking the Romans, Jesus offered him acceptance by inviting Himself to Zacchaeus' home.

What was Zacchaeus' response? He began to confess and repent of his sins. Then Jesus said, "Today salvation has come to this house" (Luke 19:9). Before Jesus met Zacchaeus' spiritual need, He met his personal need. That's the way Jesus always ministered and witnessed! It's the way we need to minister and witness, too.

Jesus understood people, knew their deepest needs, and ministered to those needs. Even though Jesus came to seek and to save the lost, He never asked people if they wanted to be saved. He was more likely to ask people if they wanted to be made well or whole or to ask, "What do you want Me to do for you?"

For evangelism to be effective, we need to understand people and know why they believe, feel, think, and act the way they do. We need to know their deepest personal and felt need. This is essential if we are to adequately personalize the Gospel.

Over 90 percent of us in today's world come from dysfunctional families. Consequently, we are hurting, lonely, isolated, depressed, and defeated. We struggle with a host of problems, as mentioned earlier.

Effective evangelism in this decade will realistically address these problems. Effective churches will provide ministries such as care, support, recovery groups, and counsel that help people overcome these problems and find deliverance, freedom, and wholeness.

For people to find God, most will need to see Him in other people first. A word of caution, however. As people tend to get their first impression of God through their parents and especially their father, we need to be careful how we present God. Those whose fathers were loving, accepting, close, and involved in their lives will probably see God in the same way. On the other hand, those whose fathers were cold and distant, uninvolved in their lives, and very demanding and judgmental, will most likely feel that God the heavenly Father is the same way. Thus many people, without being aware of it, have a faulty filter through which they have viewed God. This is why we need to be sensitive to how people feel toward Him and how we talk about Him. If, for instance, a person was physically or sexually abused by his or her father and we talk about God as the heavenly Father, that can distress rather than comfort that person. This is another reason we need to understand people if they are to find God through us.

In Christ's day, people saw God by seeing Christ. As Jesus said, "Anyone who has seen me has seen the Father" (John 14:9). For people to find God today, they need to see Him through the Christ in us (Colossians 1:27). We thus provide a much better filter through whom they can view God. We do this by being nonjudgmental, compassionate, understanding, accepting, forgiving, and loving in word and in deed. We reflect God's love by being Christ to people. If we don't do this, our words will come across as canned and cold.

Finally, in translating Scriptures today, translators are taking the dynamic equivalent rather than the formal word-for-word approach to translation. To do this successfully, the translators need to have a deep understanding of the culture in which they are working and translate the Scriptures so they have as close a meaning as possible to the original.

As Christ's representatives, we need to take the same approach in translating or interpreting the Gospel to those outside the kingdom. That is, we need to present not a word-for-word translation approach (that is, saying all the "right evangelical words") but a dynamic approach. This means we need to have a deep understanding of the people to whom we are witnessing and reflect Jesus Christ as clearly as possible. We need to not merely talk about Jesus but "be Him" to every life we touch.

Remember, Christianity is much more than a creed. It is experiencing divine love, divine acceptance, and divine forgiveness and communicating these to every life we touch.

Is That You, God?

Ever since my two sons were born, I have tucked them into bed almost every night, prayed with them, and whispered affirmations in their ears, such as,"I'm so glad that God sent you to be part of our family," "I love you devotedly," "I'm so proud of you," and so on. I often whispered these affirmations in their ears while they were sleeping. I don't know if it helped, but it never hurt.

Very early one morning, I slipped into my youngest son's bedroom through his open door. I still think he was sound asleep. He looked like an angel. It's about the only time he does. I leaned over his bed and whispered right in his ear, "O beloved of the Lord."

As quick as a flash he spun his head around and, looking up beyond me, asked in all sincerity, "Is that you, God?"

Momentarily I was speechless. When I regained my composure, I leaned over him again and whispered in his ear, "No, it's not God, but He sent me to tell you that."

That is exactly what God wants me to tell you—that He loves you absolutely, totally, and unconditionally. That's what He wants you and me to communicate to every life we touch. As we do this through our lives and through our words, may we always "speak the truth in love" (*see* Ephesians 4:15).

Discussion Questions

1. What are some of the religious words we need to avoid when sharing the Gospel?

2. How would you describe sin to a non-Christian? Justification? Sanctification? Righteousness?

3. What can we learn from Jesus' choice of words?

4. What is the difference between intellectualizing and personalizing the Gospel?

5. What is two-way communication? Why is it important?

6. What function does a person's "mental filter" play in processing all incoming information?

7. What is the key to opening closed minds?

8. How do we get people emotionally involved and avoid sticky emotionalism?

9. What makes a personal story or testimony valid?

10. How have some people seen God through a faulty filter, and how can we change that faulty view?

8
The Art of Storytelling

Jill Briscoe

It was J. R. R. Tolkien, I believe, who coined that wonderful term *eucatastrophe.* He used it to connote a sudden, unexpected, joyous, miraculous turn of grace. As such, it is a "good catastrophe," a positive upheaval, a marvelous inbreaking of blessing. According to Tolkien:

> The Birth of Christ is the eucatastrophe of Man's history. The Resurrection is the eucatastrophe of the story of the Incarnation. This story begins and ends in joy.[1]

And according to Bruce Salmon:

> Preaching is essentially an effort to communicate, transmit, transfer that experience of eucatastrophe.

> We do it by retelling the Story and by translating the experience of the Story into our own stories.[2]

What follow are three short stories which do just that—retell the Story by translating the experience of the Story into my own story.

A Smile, a Tent, and a Faith House

> The effect of specific stories may be highly personalistic. . . . Stories connect us to one another and to God because ultimately all of our individual stories are but episodes in one comprehensive Story. . . . There is something about our devotion to God which drives us to recount that experience in narrative.[3]

The girl in the bed next to me was pretty and dark. I couldn't see exactly how tall she was because the starched white sheets packaged her body so thoroughly, all that was visible was her curly coal-black hair and her lovely, bright smile.

It was nice having a smile in the bed next to me. I was nineteen, had a pain that wouldn't go away, and was scared. There were thirty beds in the ward in the old hospital at Cambridge, lined up with military precision around the austere walls. The teenager in the bed on the other side of me wasn't smiling, I observed. She was far too sick, I learned. "She's got a very serious problem," a nurse confided quietly. "All we can do is try and keep her comfortable." My stomach contracted. Was this a roundabout way of saying she was going to die? I asked the pretty girl with the smile if she knew anything about it, and she told me that the teenager was indeed dying. I took a furtive look at the pale skin, the lank hair, and the anxious, sorrowing faces of the parents sitting by her bed.

The mother was holding the too-slim hand that had been reluctantly given permission to be outside the sheets. "You've got to be dying to have a hand outside the sheet in this place," I whispered to the girl with the smile. She smiled back gravely.

The next day the teenager had gone. But just where had she gone, my nineteen-year-old inquiring mind wanted to know. Because she was in the cubical next to me, I had caught sight of her still body and with that momentary glimpse had become a believer in life after death. I had never seen a dead body before, and seeing the "house" she had inhabited lying so very still and quiet and so totally bereft of movement seemed to me to have no reasonable explanation at all other than to believe she had vacated it!

She, the pale, blue-eyed, sweet one, cheated of her adulthood, who cried a lot and stroked her mother's face, had most definitely gone. The rather archaic and prosaic phrase "the dear departed" made sense for the first time. It was just as if she had left her impermanent "tent" behind her and had pitched camp!

I was quite unaware that this picture of a tent which sprung to my mind was a biblical one, but then I was unaware of anything biblical whatsoever, never having opened a Bible or gone to church, except for a few cursory visits, or as far as I could remember met anyone else who had!

The girl with the smile was watching me. Her face was grave today, but even in repose, joy lit up her eyes and invited me to trust her. Seeking an escape from the sobering deathly event that had just occurred, I began to tell her my story.

"I'm a student far from home and feeling pretty miserable about it," I confided. "I developed this insistent sharp pain in my stomach. The college authorities suspected appendicitis and rushed me off to be packaged for healing.

That's how I ended up here. This is my very first time in a hospital," I confessed. "It's pretty frightening," I added, "when you see people dying all over the place!"

The girl with the smile didn't answer immediately. She had a thoughtful look about her that I couldn't read. I discovered she had a pretty name to match the smile. It was Janet. She began to tell me her story. "I am a nurse," she said. "I was on duty one night and lifted a very heavy patient. Losing my balance, I damaged my back and had to have a spinal fusion." She went on to tell me how she loved nursing and wondered if she would be able to continue her vocation. I wondered why she wasn't more concerned. I'd be furious with fate if that had happened to me. Something told me she didn't believe in fate!

Her story caught my interest. Being a teacher in training, I was interested in stories. This one sounded like a good one! It had an introduction and plot, and the tension was mounting. The element of conflict was there. I wondered just how her story would end. All my favorite stories resolved the conflicts and had happy endings. I hoped very much hers would, too.

Glancing to my left, I saw that the still "tent" of our companion had been whisked away and was presumably on its way to be totally dismantled. She had had a kidney problem, we learned. So had I! Imagine my consternation. Now I began to wonder how my story was going to end! I voiced my concern. "There doesn't seem to be any real danger of your tent being dismantled," I was assured by the staff nurse, a sort of disinterested starched paragon of cleanliness who patrolled the ward rather like a warden. "But you never know, do you?" I said to Janet anxiously, when she had moved on to the next prisoner (sorry, patient). "It sort of makes you think," I added.

Then with a glib remark (in case she thought I was afraid of death), I rattled on, "Actually the admitting nurse asked me what denomination I belong to, which didn't give me very much confidence! It was as if they wanted to be prepared." My voice trailed away, but Janet jumped in, "And what did you say?" "Well, I just said I was a-a-Christian," I replied with a cocky grin, thinking my smart answer would amuse her as it had amused me. "And are you?" she shot back. "Am I what?" I asked, startled. "A Christian." "Of course," I retorted. "I'm English, aren't I?"

She laughed then, and I was glad. It sort of released the growing tension between us. I hadn't liked her question. Religion was not a hot topic of conversation, as far as I was concerned. And certainly not today. It made me nervous in the light of present events. I rolled over in bed so I could end the dialogue. Then I began to worry. Perhaps Janet knew something I didn't know. After all, she was a nurse. Maybe one of the other nurses had confided some vital piece of information to her, just like the one who had confided the information to me about the teenager's condition.

I wondered what denomination the poor girl had belonged to. Did it matter? I asked myself. And if it did, how do you know if you belong to the right one? I took myself sternly in hand. *How morbid can you get, Jill?* I lectured myself. Death wasn't on my schedule for at least another fifty years, at the very least! Restlessly, looking for a distraction, I turned back toward Janet. She was lying flat, as usual, her dark, curly head propped up on the plump pillow, her pretty arms quite out of the healing package, and in her hands she held a Bible! My stomach did a complete somersault. What on earth was she doing reading a Bible? I made a quick mental calculation. It wasn't even Sunday! And the Bible was BIG. I mean really BIG! She hadn't struck me as shortsighted, either! The most amazing thing of all was the smile. It was big, it was bright, it was brilliant! She was obviously, unashamedly and without apology, delighted with her occupation.

Shocked into inquiry, Janet answered my earnest questions as best as she could. It was just as if she began to build me a "faith house" to live in. First she laid a good foundation of biblical facts—things I knew but had never really thought about till then. Shocked out of my trivial thinking by facing the issues of life and death, I was ready to listen.

"God made us with a capacity to know Him," she said. "But sin had created a barrier between us, our sin." (I was glad she said "our" sin and not "your" sin!) That identification helped me to listen and not turn her off. "Jesus, God in human form, had come to earth to live and die for us. We should thank Him personally for this incredible act of self-sacrificial love," which she assured me was the only way to be forgiven. We needed to give ourselves to Him. If we did, she promised, God would give Himself to us!

Having laid the foundation of faith and built the frame of the Gospel story firmly upon it, she began to fill in the structure, giving illustrations of people who had become believers. In other words, she fitted some "windows" into place. Windows let in the light and are like illustrations in a talk.

I was fascinated, not least by her unadulterated joy as she shared "the greatest story ever told" with me. Having built a "faith house" for her new friend, she invited me to enter it to enjoy all that God had in store. Praying a simple prayer, I was able to step shyly over the threshold and meet Jesus inside!

In the years that followed I became a storyteller myself, roaming my world, building faith houses for anyone who would give me half a chance and listen to my story. Anyone can witness using stories. All you need is a listener, a good tale, and a little practice. The Holy Spirit will do the rest!

A Bowling Alley, a Hairpiece, and a Bottle of Wine

> Stories can bring new life to a gospel message which is otherwise all too familiar. Stories can help to bridge the distance between the worldview of the Bible and our own. Stories can reduce or even eliminate the distance between the pulpit and the pew. Stories can serve as a balancing corrective to an overemphasis on relational argument by appealing to the emotions and the will. Stories can function effectively in a visual context because they enable people to see with the mind, imagination, and heart.[4]

My seventh-grade English class had begun. We were asked to write an essay about our vacation. I didn't know where to start. "Make a list of things about your vacation," suggested the teacher. I did, eight of them. "Now put them in order and write about each point," the teacher instructed us. And so I began. The advice came in very handy forty years later!

It was winter in Wisconsin. The wind howled, the snow looked like white sand dunes, and I was apprehensive. I was supposed to give an inspirational talk at a service club that evening. The club met in a party room at a bowling alley. While the men discussed their project, I was supposed to speak to their wives. *Now just what do I say and how do I say it?* I wondered. On the one hand, it was a wonderful opportunity to explain the Gospel to a group of people outside church walls. On the other hand, I was at a loss to know how to begin and how to hold their attention. I worked long and hard on a "sermon."

A comparatively new arrival in the U.S.A., I was still adjusting to driving on the "wrong" (sorry, right) side of the road. Ice and snow were elements I had not encountered in such dangerous quantities, so as I backed out of our garage in a near blizzard, I went straight into a ditch! A kindly neighbor dug me out, but by the time I got to my rendezvous, my hairpiece was decidedly askew and I was, to say the least, flustered!

Finding my way to a side room through the skittles and bowling alleys, I discovered about seventy women who were finishing the first half of their "entertainment." I apparently was billed to be their second half! I thought briefly and not very kindly about the deacon at our new church who had let me in for this and decided I would check out, as he had put it, "these 'wonderful opportunities' to share the Gospel" a little more closely next time!

The first half was over, and the women were happy. Very happy! They had been experiencing a wine tasting. The lecture given by an expert was complete with action to fit the talk! At least there was a smile on everyone's face! I scrapped my well-prepared message and frantically wondered what on earth to say. Walking up to the speaker, I stuck out my hand and offered a good old traditional handshake, only to find an empty bottle of wine put into it by the presenter. There was a little left in it, and I suppose he meant for me to join the crew and sample it.

Standing there in front of that rather extraordinary audience with my storm-swept hairdo (my hairpiece wasn't quite over one eye) and the almost-empty bottle of wine in my hand, I reflected on the laugh my husband and I would enjoy later on. But later on was later on, and here and now must be dealt with. "What can I say, Lord?" I prayed, sending an emergency FAX heavenward. I seemed to hear Him say, "Tell them a story." But what story? I looked at the wine bottle and decided to use it as a visual aid. The only biblical story that sprung to mind was the story of the wedding at Cana from John, chapter two, and so, remembering my seventh-grade English lesson, I made a mental list of all the facts I could remember and launched forth, making the story as applicable as I could along the way.

"Look here," I began, holding up my visual aid. "What a shame, the wine's run out! That reminds me of a story I heard about a wedding where that happened. Jesus Christ was a guest. He wasn't the governor of the feast, so He didn't do anything about the problem till He was asked to, but when His mother told Him about it, He instructed the servants to fill the tall water pots with water and turned it into wine! When the people drank it, they were amazed and said it was far better than any of the wine they had had before." Having told my story, I began to apply it.

"It's funny, isn't it," I said, "how often the wine seems to run out of marriage, even though everything seemed to be wonderful at the wedding. Relationships can become flat and insipid. The problem is," I explained, "Jesus may have been invited to the wedding, but only as guest and not as governor!"

I put the bottle down. I didn't need any help to keep their attention now. I had begun to tell their story, and they identified. Heartened, I explained how Christ can make such a difference when He is given His rightful place in our lives. "He can turn the water into wine," I assured them. "Your relationships can be better than any you've had before," I insisted. Here and there a head nodded, wide eyes grew wider. Some were filled with longing and some with cynicism, but at least I had their ear. Whenever I felt I was losing them, I fitted a window into the talk! I wove some ministories among the truth about marriages God had governed and sweetened, making them "better than any that had gone before." A long time later, when the other people had gone home, a young woman stayed to talk. She sat still and intent, listening to THE STORY all over again. The true story of the One who can still work relational miracles today. I told her more stories of the power of God in the family, and finally she went home, a new creature in Christ.

Backing happily out of the bowling alley parking lot, I nearly went into a ditch for the second time in one evening! But then, this was Wisconsin, and that's the way it is in winter. It didn't matter. It had been a wonderful, wonderful day!

A Hairy Dream and a Strong Man

> [A story] must be conveyed with enthusiasm, spontaneity, and freedom. Only as we have mastered the story, and been mastered by it, can the story come alive.[5]

If the Gospel is the greatest story ever told, we must ask ourselves a hard question: Why isn't it being told to the people who need to hear it? Is it because we are not convinced it's all that great? Are we perhaps convincing the convinced, fishing in a swimming pool? The fish Jesus sent us to catch are in muddy pools and streams outside our church boundaries. Believing we needed to creatively find the right audience, a group of professional women intent on fishing where the fish were had generated an unusual opportunity and invited me to speak.

I was speaking to more than seventy beauticians, treated by their Christian clients to a Thank You Dinner. We'd presented a wonderful program of contemporary music, a few tips on "How to Handle Stress," and had had a good laugh at an extremely funny skit put on by five hairdressers, showing us a typical day in the life of typical clients in a typical beauty parlor. Now it was my turn!

"Let me tell you a 'hairy' story," I began. Eyebrows raised. A bright-blonde coifed head half turned in my direction. A friend at the front table in the smart restaurant glanced furtively at her guest. "It's about Samson," I added. *Very little name recognition,* I observed. *Some of these women haven't a clue who he is! Maybe they think he owns a salon.* "He went to the beauty shop to get his hair cut," I continued gamely, interest definitely generated, I thought with satisfaction. I'd managed to establish a point of identification, a bridge to these people who lived in a different sphere than me.

"The beauty operator who cut Samson's hair was called Delilah," I confided, realizing I needed to lay out the story and not presume they had heard it before. "She gave him a short back and sides, as he lay in her lap. A lot more than he bargained for!" Two rather wild-looking girls, young, bright-eyed, and bushy-tailed, stood up (*Oh no, they're leaving,* I thought), but they were just turning their chairs around to get a better view! *Good! Develop the plot, Jill,* I urged myself.

"This particular appointment had a devastating effect on Samson," I said soberly. "It drained all his strength, and he became extraordinarily weak. He was dragged off Delilah's lap, made to look like a fool in public, suffered terribly, and ended up committing suicide." Now I had them! Those who wouldn't look and still had their backs to me were listening. Oh, yes they were! They didn't want me to know it, but their body language told me anyway. They were suddenly very, very still. "All over a haircut?" I could almost hear them saying incredulously!

"Now, Lord," I whispered, "where do we go from here?" I thought about my husband. (It's quite amazing what thoughts go weaving their way in and out of a story even while you're actually telling it!) I love to say I peek around the corner of the verses of Scripture to see who is standing in the shadows. This way you can smell the smells and observe whose aunt, sister, friend, or enemy is lurking around the place. My husband lovingly kids me as

I fly out the door for yet one more storytelling challenge, asking, "Well, Jill, are you going to peek around the corner of the verse today?" "Yes," I reply cheerily. "Well," his eyes twinkle, "don't go all the way round the block!"

He means, "Use your imagination, Jill, by all means, but make sure the truth is not compromised." In other words, use your imagination on your observations, applications, and illustrations rather than on the interpretation of the passage! Story alone won't do it. Proclamation has to be part of it if people are to understand their need for Christ. I came back to earth. Having won a hearing with my imagination in storytelling, I realized I needed to tell the story over again and make sure the women listening to me understood the truth and the application.

It is not for nothing that God calls us His children, I thought, looking around that particular muddy stream. Kids go for stories as much as fish go for worms! I took a deep breath and continued, "Let me tell you the story all over again."

"There really was a man called Samson who had extremely long hair. His story is in the Bible. He really had no business getting it cut. You see, Samson had a very distinctive hairstyle. It was called the 'Nazarite Look.' He had vowed he'd never change it, because it was symbolic of all he was as a person and all he believed about God. He believed God had a wonderful plan for his life, and it was his responsibility to find and fulfill it."

Uh-oh, I was losing some of my story circle. I'd better do something! Perhaps it was the mention of the Bible that was a bit threatening. A little humor might help here. I slipped in a little joke and laughter ran around the room. Praise God for humor, especially at a "dry place." *Blessed are the humorous, for they shall earn the right to continue their story,* I thought.

"God did have a plan for Samson's life," I plowed on, "but so did Satan." Instant reaction! Now I had their attention again, but a block had appeared in their thinking. It had to be removed before they could hear the rest of the story. I didn't need to be too clever to realize that the mention of Satan introduced a controversial element into the situation: a little smirk, a touch of contempt or amusement. I could see it all out there on those faces. I guessed that gory visuals were being conjured up of a dancing creature in red tights with horns, carrying a pitchfork! I remembered C. S. Lewis had said that the devil doesn't mind if we ignore him or are obsessed by him. Either extreme works to his advantage. I needed to demythologize him. This called for me to weave in a subplot. I had the best villain I could possibly ask for to generate new interest. Most really great stories have a bad guy, you know!

So I tried to explain the one behind all the evil in the world in believable terms. Recognition dawned on a few faces. "Yes," I mused, "you've met him, haven't you!"

"Satan has a plan for your life as well as God," I informed them. "His plan is to thwart God's good intentions for your life." Actually I said, "mess up," not "thwart." I was struggling to speak the language of these people, to listen to my story myself, as I was telling it (very important) and ask myself, *Is this so clear a little child could get it?* I remembered Winston Churchill had once said, "I regard the habit of using a long word when a short one will do utterly reprehensible!" I returned to the story line.

"God's plan was really working well," I said, having briefly explained it. "But Samson went and got his hair cut! He compromised his beliefs and acted against his conscience and he was captured, tortured, and died." Next I invited them inside my life and shared how easy it is to be like Samson. "My parents brought me up to believe in God and know right from wrong, but I got my hair cut! I blew it, as Samson did, doing things I knew were wrong. I brought a lot of suffering on myself. When I was nineteen, I asked God to help me overcome my enemies. He did!"

Now it was still in the room. A girl nervously took out a cigarette case and lit up. Another powdered her nose. The majority just sat and looked at me. I prayed hard, "Oh, Lord, help me now." As gently as I could, I asked them if they had ever compromised their beliefs as Samson had. I inquired if some Delilah had cut their hair, tempting them to renounce their faith. They needed to be reassured that God would forgive them, and they could return to Him without fear of vengeance. "God doesn't get even with us," I assured them. "His plan waits. We can be part of it." I explained briefly how Christ had made a way for us to be forgiven and restored to fellowship and said I would pray a prayer on their behalf if they liked. Heads bent—frosted heads, auburn heads, gray-blue heads, even purple heads! *Oh, God,* I prayed silently, *see them. You know what's going on. I don't need to know.* Then out loud, "Lord, I believe You have a plan for me. I need to be forgiven for my sin. Come into my heart. Like Samson, I vow a vow promising to love and obey You. Help me to have Your supernatural strength to overcome the difficult things in my life. Amen."

The meeting was over. A line of women waited to say precious things. "I never heard; I never knew." "That story's *really* in the Bible? Where?" "What about my handicapped child? Is that in the plan?" "Why didn't God save Samson after his hair grew again?" (Nobody ever likes the hero to die!)

Much later in my hotel room, waiting for sleep to come, I thought about the "hairy" evening and the hairier story of Samson. *Only a story could have done it,* I thought, and I thanked the Master Storyteller, Jesus, who I knew smiled at me and nodded in agreement!

Discussion Questions

1. Why are stories so effective?

2. Does storytelling take a gift, or can anyone tell a story? What do you think? What does Jill Briscoe say?

3. What portion(s) of each story had the most impact on you? Why?

4. With which of the characters in the first story can you identify? The second story? The third story?

5. Why was Jill Briscoe glad that Janet said "our" sin and not "your" sin?

6. What are "windows," and why are they helpful?

7. Can you think of situations where one of these stories would probably be effective?

8. What stories do you have to tell? What stories could you tell that you have been unwilling to tell thus far in your life?

9. What made Jesus' stories (e.g., His parables) so powerful? Think, for example, of His use of agricultural stories in a largely agricultural land.

10. What gets in the way of telling stories? Are we too often in a hurry, needing to communicate truth in brief but abstract sentences? Are we simply out of practice? Are there other reasons we don't often tell stories?

9
The Art of Handling Objections/ Defending the Faith

Charles "Chic" Shaver

Tom Phillips, president of Raytheon Corporation, shared his faith in Christ with Charles Colson, who had been one of the closest advisors to President Richard Nixon. He handed him a copy of C. S. Lewis' *Mere Christianity*. Out in his car, after leaving Phillips' house, Colson prayed. He was not yet a believer, but he was sensing an inner urge to surrender.

During the next days, while vacationing in a Maine cottage overlooking the sea, Charles Colson raised his objections to Christianity and found answers in *Mere Christianity*. More than a Lewis book, however, the Spirit of God was drawing him. On a Friday morning Colson prayed, "Lord Jesus, I believe You. I accept You. Please come into my life. I commit it to You." And there was peace.[1]

What Colson did in raising objections to faith in Christ is common. Most of these he raised while alone, after leaving Tom Phillips, and he thought them through to an answer. Often, however, persons hearing of their need for Christ will raise their objections in front of the witness. Sometimes the objections are honest intellectual problems and sometimes a diversionary tactic to avoid facing personal issues. Yet there is an art to be learned in handling these objections that will make witnessing more effective.

The Spiritual Realities

We face objections unrealistically if we assume the problems raised are rooted only in human questioning and answered only in human reasoning. Our attempt to introduce people to Jesus Christ is a struggle "not against flesh and blood, but against . . . the spiritual forces of evil in the heavenly realms" (Ephesians 6:12). Only God's armor will equip us for battle.

Though our human skills will never be the means by which a person is converted, this should not discourage us—rather it should encourage us. Jesus said, "No one can come to me unless the Father who sent me draws him" (John 6:44), but the *Father is drawing* people. Jesus promised the Holy Spirit would "convict the world of guilt in regard to sin and righteousness and judgment" (John 16:8). The Lord implied God was at work in the world preparing a harvest but needing workers when He said, "The harvest is plentiful but the workers are few" (Matthew 9:37). The task to which He calls us in light of the harvest, plentiful and ready, is a decidedly spiritual task: "Ask the Lord of the harvest, therefore, to send out workers into his harvest field" (Matthew 9:38). Paul recognized that though God uses people to bring in the harvest, God's grace is the primary ingredient. His formula was, "I planted the seed, Apollos watered it, but God made it grow" (1 Corinthians 3:6). As we share Christ with others, we may be sure a drawing Father, a convicting Spirit, and a burdened Savior are preparing a harvest. We shall cooperate in prayer and obedience.

Prospect Receptivity

The constraints of time will not permit me to personally witness to every unsaved person I know within the next week. I will need to make choices as to whom I shall speak about the Savior. I may go to the most resistant or the most receptive. Both desperately need the Gospel, but I have a much greater chance for a positive response when I go to the most receptive.

Early in my Christian life, I tended to group all people into two categories: saved or unsaved. I thought all unsaved people needed only one thing—to be saved—and I dealt with all unsaved the same way. Now I see that different unsaved people need to be approached differently, depending on their openness. Let's assume three unsaved friends may be characterized as "not open," "open," and "hungry." If I have time to deal with only one of the three this coming Thursday, I would tend to share the Gospel with the one characterized as "hungry," because there is the greatest chance that person will come to Christ. In a sense, I am trying to cooperate with the drawing of the Father already evident in that life.

James Engel and Wilbert Norton helped me understand

the importance of prospect receptivity in the development of their Spiritual Decision Process Model.[2] In that model, individuals are ranked by their knowledge, interest in, or response to the Gospel. A person who has passed through the stage of "initial awareness of Gospel" to a "positive attitude toward Gospel" is a better prospect for receiving Christ than the person who still is only at the "initial awareness of Gospel" stage. An individual at the "personal problem recognition" stage is even more likely to receive Christ than the individual at "positive attitude toward Gospel." The one with personal-problem recognition has not only understood the Gospel and come to like the Gospel but now has a strong felt need for change. Because of this combination of factors, this person is most likely to accept Christ.

A good prospect for receiving the Gospel is a person moving toward God instead of away from God and experiencing an insecurity-producing situation in life (marriage, a new job, a new neighborhood). It is obvious that a choice of the best prospects with which to share the Gospel will greatly reduce objections to the Gospel. In a sense they have been prepared, and many objections have already been resolved.

I do not rule out going to less than the best prospects. Right now I am experiencing a burden for Sid,[3] a man I have known for more than ten years. I do not see any indication of good prospect status in him, but the Spirit has so burdened my heart for him that I shall find a way to get to him with the Gospel. Normally, however, the *pattern* will be to go to the best prospects first.

The Mind-set of the Witness

The effective witness lives with the determination to win people to an allegiance to Jesus Christ. Yet the determined witness is not in bondage. Like a good fisherman, the witness throws out bait and then speaks to those who respond. It is a relief to discover that if the prospect shows no interest and does not take the bait, the witness may legitimately drop the subject. However, everyone I know who is being used by God in personal evangelism has an attitude of expectancy to discover interested people.

The witness is not a winner of arguments but a winner of people to Christ. The witness is going to hungry and needy people with joyous, life-changing news. The prospect is not an enemy to be fought but a person to be loved and won. It's not so much like arguing a case in a courtroom as wooing and winning a girl to be your wife.

To create a positive atmosphere, you may meet objections with, "I'm glad you said that." You are sincerely glad your prospect has the freedom to express inner feelings to you. The fact that your prospect is raising questions is a sign that you have his or her attention. Your positive attitude and evidence that you are not threatened by objections helps your prospect relax and drains off the tendency to argumentativeness.

Several things may be done with arguments or objections: they may be precluded, delayed, or met. James Kennedy has urged us to preclude arguments by leading prospects to agree with Scripture before they can raise objections.[4] His *Evangelism Explosion* Gospel outline is so effective because it has been structured to meet so many issues that are problem areas for prospects. For example, Kennedy deals with God's love and mercy before God's justice and righteousness, because he found more people believed in God's mercy than in His justice. Once the point is made about God's love and mercy, Kennedy follows with a statement like this: "But the *same Bible* that teaches that God is loving and merciful also teaches us that God is just and righteous." He has helped preclude an argument about

God holding people accountable for their sins, because the message of mercy from the same source, the Bible, was gladly accepted. It would be inconsistent for prospects to reject God's justice since they accepted God's mercy.

There are times when an objection can be delayed or postponed. My favorite witnessing tool is an adaptation of Kennedy's *Evangelism Explosion* outline. Seventy percent of questions raised when I am sharing the Gospel are issues that are dealt with later in the presentation. I am able to say to the prospect, "That's a good question, and there's an answer to that in what I discovered about the Gospel and am sharing with you. If you'll hold that a bit, you'll see the answer in a moment." If an issue is raised that you will not be covering in your sharing of the Gospel and the issue is extraneous, you might say, "That's a good question, and I'd be glad to discuss it with you. If you don't mind, would you hold it till we're finished with what we're talking about? If you'll bring it up again later, we can take a look at it together." I have the right to do this, since I have previously gained permission to share what I've discovered about the Gospel. Of course, you can't delay the question if it's essential rather than extraneous.

If an objection is raised and it needs an answer, but you do not know the answer, be honest with your prospect. You might say, "I'm not sure I know the answer to that. If you'll let me do some checking on it, I'll get back to you with some information." It's called "research and return."

The end result of many objections is that they get off the discussion of the subject—which is the prospect's relationship with God. We may not owe an unbeliever an answer to each challenge to God's will and Word, but we do owe the person we are calling on "to keep the communication process open long enough to 'put the Gospel home.' "[5] Donald A. Abdon proposes a four-step method for handling objections:

Step 1: Determine What the Real Objection Is
Few people tell you what they really think. Realize you are dealing with a non-Christian who is subject to self-deception without being aware of that fact.
Step 2: Accept the Objection
You do not agree with the objection, but you acknowledge the existence of the objection and keep the communication open. You might say, "I know a lot of people who think that."
Step 3: Reassert the Subject
Handle the objection with two or three short sentences and get back to the subject. Pick the key word out of the objection and go back into the real subject where the prospect came out.
Step 4: Reaffirm the Gospel

The Reverend Abdon places most objections into one of seven categories: substitutes for Christ, self-righteousness, blaming other people, the organized church, intellectual difficulties, the surroundings ("I can't stand to be in a crowd"), and life itself.

For example, if a person objects, "All religions are the same," you *determine the real objection* and see this as fitting under the category "substitutes for Christ." You might answer, "I know there are a lot of people who think that and there are certain similarities in religions" (*accept the objection*). "But there is one basic difference. A religion is something people do or practice. Christianity isn't just a religion; it's a faith" (*reassert the subject*). "Christ is the center of that faith. To be a Christian is to know and believe in a Person—Jesus Christ. He's the One we came to talk to you about." Then, *reaffirm the Gospel*. Note that we use his concept of religion to get back to the real subject, and we do that by defining the word *religion* differently. Go back into the subject where the individual came out.[6]

As a witness, keep your motives pure. Under certain objections, you will be tempted to prove your prospect wrong so you can save yourself embarrassment. Just the opposite should be done—do all you can to absorb the embarrassment yourself and save your prospect discomfort.

I was trying to witness to Wil. I'd had a several-year acquaintance with him, and his wife was a member of our church. I asked him, "Have you ever heard of the Four Spiritual Laws?" Abruptly he responded, "No, and I don't want to." I was embarrassed, but I realized if I allowed the moment to stand with only those feelings around it, all future attempts to discuss Christianity with Wil would be negative experiences. So to relieve his embarrassment, I said, "Wil, I believe you are a thinking person. If you ever decide you want to talk about this, please feel free to raise the subject with me. I want to be your friend."

A great deal of objection to the Gospel is avoided if the witness has gotten really close to the prospect and deeply identifies with him. I was trying to witness to Jake. He had lived a rough, sin-filled life and was dying of cancer. I asked his son how I could approach him. The son told me to stress my life *at its worst* before I came to Christ and his dad would understand. I did, and Jake opened up. He prayed, invited Christ to become Savior, and asked for baptism. The deeper identification overcame his previous reluctance. Two days later he went out to meet the Lord.

When I call on people with the hope of sharing Christ, my mind-set expects that God will work. Besides the possibility they will ask me difficult questions, I pray God will cause them to ask me the right questions. Upon returning from Dr. Kennedy's personal evangelism training in Fort Lauderdale, I announced to my seminary students that I would go calling with any of them who had a prospect. A student asked me to call on his contact Jim. No matter that I hadn't won anyone with this approach yet! I sat in Jim's living room, nervous, debating how to get into a spiritual discussion. I wanted to ask him, "Jim, have you come to a place in your spiritual life where you know for certain that if you died tonight you'd go to heaven?" I didn't see an opening, but I was praying as we talked. Suddenly Jim said, "Reverend Shaver, our son died in infancy. If my wife and I are privileged to get to heaven, will we know our little boy as our little boy?" Remember my earlier prayer, "O God, cause them to ask me the right questions"? That night I had the opportunity to pray for Jim and his wife, along with seven other adult relatives, to accept Christ, and it was the first time I'd shared the Gospel since returning from Kennedy's school. God does work as we trust Him!

Intellectual Objections

Though some objections may be precluded and others delayed, there are some genuine intellectual objections that must be answered if we are to progress. They are questions about essential truths. Paul Little made it a practice of speaking on secular campuses. He noted several basic questions that were being asked. He recorded these in his powerful little book *How to Give Away Your Faith*.[7] I still find these helpful today.

One of these questions he heard frequently was, "What about the heathen?" Or, "What about the people who have never heard of Jesus Christ? Will they be condemned to hell?" This seems to me an intellectually fair question that needs an answer because it raises the issue in many minds, "Is God fair?" I've had this question raised a number of times. I always deal with it as quickly as possible and then return to the Gospel. Drawing on Little's suggestion, I take the questioner to Romans 2:1: "You, therefore, have no excuse, you who pass judgment on someone else, for at whatever point you judge the other, you are condemning yourself, because you who pass judgment do the same things." Then I set up a hypothetical case:

> Imagine, John, a primitive tribe. They've never heard of Christ. One man sitting around the camp fire says to the others, "It's not right for you to beat your wives." The next night, his wife puts too much salt on his meat, and he beats her. He is lost, not because he rejected a Christ of whom he has never heard, but because he has set a standard of judgment for others and violated his own standard himself.

The times I can remember using this explanation, it has satisfied the hearer. Then we continue with the Gospel.

> But John, our concern should not be primarily some pagan who has never heard of Christ but you and me, who have heard of Christ. The question that so moved me is, How can I find God and eternal life through Christ?

Let me suggest several other arguments and Paul Little's answers in thumbnail sketch. Please note that some responses only partially answer the problems raised, but all are helpful:

1. *Is Christ the only way to God?*
   As Christians, we have no other option because Christ has said no man can come to the Father but by Him (John 14:6). Although one may choose to believe what he wishes, he has no right to redefine

Christianity in his own terms. Some laws are socially determined, like the fine for running a stop sign. The law of gravity cannot be set or suspended by vote of a city council. We discern these laws and moral laws from what God has revealed.

2. *Why do the innocent suffer?*
   a) God gave man freedom to obey or disobey God, and evil came into the universe through man's disobedience. One person's actions affect others.
   b) What about the evil in each person? If God decreed all evil stamped out of the universe at midnight, which of us would be here at 1:00 A.M.?
   c) God has met the problem of evil in the coming and death of Christ.

3. *How can miracles be possible?*
   a) If God is God, miracles are logical.
   b) If Christ is not the truth, is He a liar, a lunatic, or a legend?
   c) Remember that scientific method and measure are not the only ways to discover the truth. You've never seen three feet of love or two pounds of justice, but we don't deny their reality.

4. *I don't believe the Bible.*
   a) Which errors do you have in mind?
   b) "Do you understand its main message—how to receive eternal life?" He may respond that he doesn't believe in eternal life. You reply, "I'm not asking what you believe but what you understand. It would be unintellectual to reject the

world's most important book without understanding its main message. May I share what the Bible says about how to receive eternal life?"[8]

5. *Won't a good moral life get me into heaven?*
   Imagine the human race lined up on the west coast of the United States, and at the crack of the gun they all jump into the Pacific to swim to Hawaii. Some swim farther than others, but all drown. The religions of the world are swimming instructions, but our problem is not a problem of knowing how to live; it's a problem of finding the power to live. Christ gives that power.

Of course, it would be possible to list many other objections. One must realize that some questions are asked as a diversion when a witness gets too close. Remember the intellectual question raised by the woman at the well (John 4:17–20) when Jesus became personal about her relationship to men. Jesus' response to her question took her quickly back to main issues (John 4:21–24). Let us lead those to whom we witness back to the main issue.

Emotional Objections

Often when a Christian endeavors to witness, the prospect will respond about some hurting experience of life. He or she may tell of a church that caused disappointment or a hypocrite who caused hurt. They may refer to a minister who has gone bad. I try to empathize with their feelings without trying to get into details. It is impossible for me to know the real details, since I wasn't there. Usually I can say, "It's sad when people disappoint us. We don't want to be the kind of people who disappoint someone else." I may point out that the early church had to face the same problems. In Acts 8 we read about Simon Peter and Simon the sorcerer. One was genuine and one was phony. The church then and we today must be discerning enough to tell the genuine from the phony.

Sometimes the prospect, sensing the love of the Christian, will want to share a hurt of life that is not related to Christian faith and not a matter of blaming God. In all these cases of sharing emotional objections, I prefer they be shared earlier in the discussion with the prospect to clear the air, so to speak, before I begin sharing the Gospel.

Objections About Living the Christian Life

The Gospel has been shared. The prospect has been open and kind. All objections of an intellectual and emotional nature seem satisfied. The person is finally asked to accept Christ. The prospect hesitates and then objects, "I'm afraid I can't live it!" Recently, after I witnessed to a young adult, John, he told me that very thing. I responded that Christ wasn't asking him to live the Christian life on his strength but was seeking entrance to his life so that Christ living within would give him a new source of power (Revelation 3:20; 1 John 4:4; Galatians 2:20). God promised us we would not be tempted beyond what we could bear, but God would provide a way out (1 Corinthians 10:13). When we sin, we should immediately take the matter to God through Christ, who speaks in our defense for forgiveness and cleansing (1 John 2:1; 1:9).

Further, I pointed out that a person driving to the next city might have a flat tire. He might make one of three decisions. He might give up. He might drive on the flat until he arrives at the next gas station, needing a new tire or a new wheel and perhaps major repair to the underside of the car. Or he might stop the car, remove the flat, put on the spare, and arrive at his destination with hardly an interruption in the trip. So a Christian surprised into sin should not give up or continue until the next church service, by which to receive a major spiritual overhaul. The Christian should stop immediately, take the matter to God through Christ in confession, receive forgiveness and restoration, and continue with hardly an interruption in the spiritual journey. Often, when Christianity is presented as genuine, livable, and Christ-centered, the prospect is ready to pray to receive Christ.

One of the most common experiences I'm having today when calling in homes and challenging people to accept Christ is hearing responses like this one: Greg told me he had once accepted Christ. Because of that, he knew he was going to heaven, but then he named the sins in which he was living and admitted he was living for the devil. I was shocked because I understand that to receive Christ by grace and faith should result in good works (Ephesians 2:8–10) and that continued, willful sinning is inconsistent with being born of God (1 John 3:4–10). I also knew that within Christianity there were theological differences in the defining of sin, the presence of sin in the life of the Christian, and the effect of sinning on an individual's relationship with God and salvation. Understanding the perspective from which Greg is speaking, I would probably avoid emphasis on doctrinal differences, but I could ask him one or all of these questions:

1. Are you now in fellowship with Jesus Christ?
2. What has Jesus Christ done in your life this week that indicates your relationship with Him is what it ought to be?
3. Is your relationship with Christ as meaningful and satisfying as you wish it to be?

If Greg were responsive to these questions in a way that indicated spiritual hunger, my decision question to him would be, "Would you like to renew your relationship with

Jesus Christ?" When this prospect was open and tender, I would explain salvation as a *relationship* with Christ that needs continuation (Colossians 2:6). I'm happy to say that several days after our discussion, Greg made a fresh commitment to Christ and later joined the church.

Sometimes objections are answered by modeling. Mike accepted Christ on October 22 when a friend shared the Gospel with him. His wife, Sara, was reluctant. She did, however, begin attending church with Mike. On the following February 20, I went to Sara with several people from our church, and she prayed to receive Christ. I asked her what had convinced her, and she said she saw such a change in her husband. On March 18 they both joined the church by profession of their faith.

These questions raised as the Spirit probes hearts deeply can be especially significant. I had shared the Gospel with a young couple, Fred and Patty, on a cold February night. Our discussion had been very thorough, but Patty was filled with questions, having attended church only six or eight times in her life. When I urged them to accept Christ and His gift of eternal life, Patty asked if she would have to tithe to go to heaven. I was puzzled at the question, but she explained she had heard only one sermon at our church, and it had been on tithing. I replied, "Patty, I don't want to tell you if you have to tithe or not. I am asking you to accept Jesus Christ as Savior and Lord. If you begin following Jesus as your Lord and He tells you that you should tithe, would you?" She thought a moment and said, "Yes."

Again I asked Fred and Patty if they would accept Christ. She raised another objection: "If I accept Christ tonight, will I be in one minute as you are after twenty years of being a Christian?" I explained that you could be really alive and young and all you were supposed to be at one day old spiritually but not all you would be after twenty years of maturing. Fearfully, I again asked them to accept Christ. They beautifully prayed, received the Savior, in a few weeks began tithing, and shortly thereafter joined the church by profession of faith. Today Fred serves on the church board, and they have a reputation for godliness. Patty's questions came not from rebellion but from honest searching.

The Issue of the Will

Paul witnessed to King Agrippa. Agrippa raised objection to accepting Christ, but the issue was purely his unwillingness to surrender to a higher power (Acts 26:28). The barrier of the intellect and the emotions may be crossed, but the barrier of the will is the highest of all. A few days ago I shared Christ with Roy, a young adult. He said, "I have been independent so long. Since eighteen I've been on my own. It's hard to surrender to another." He has not yet responded. He promised to think about it, but he has seen the issue: surrender to Another!

I told Betty of Christ's power to save. We looked at Revelation 3:19, 20: "So . . . repent. Here I am! I stand at the door and knock. If anyone hears my voice and opens the door, I will come in and eat with him. . . ." She prayed. I heard her invite Jesus in with words. After the prayer, in anger she said, "Jesus didn't come in. It doesn't work for me." Then she asked her divorced husband and pastor to leave the room. She admitted to me an affair with a married doctor at the hospital where she worked. She was not willing to give up the illicit relationship. I pointed out she hadn't really repented and hadn't really opened the door to Christ. She had blamed Jesus, but the issue was her will. She agreed. She wanted the doctor more than Jesus.[9]

Ron is a Harvard Ph.D. in his sixties. For most of his life he has been an atheist or an agnostic. A few years ago, he became part of a Christian support group and sensed evidence of Christian love. Then both Ron and his wife began to have serious health problems. For years he had raised objection to the Christian Gospel. Now Christian love and the failure of health broke open his proud shell of self-sufficiency. The night I shared Christ in their home all objections had melted, and Ron and Delores fell to their knees, prayed, and found Christ. Today they are vibrant members of our church. So often the intellectual questions are solved in time by love and circumstances and prayer and the Spirit.

Conclusion

Do not fear objections. You can develop a skill in handling them, and you will experience rich blessings as you see God draw people to Christ through a maze of objections. But there is so often a last objection for most people who seek Christ. As you are afraid of objections, they are afraid to pray. So when you ask them to accept Christ, offer to pray for them a model prayer that they can repeat after you if they mean it. It can still be sincere, and it relieves their fear—and they can be truly saved.

Perhaps your witness has ended, and the last issue most apparent is their objection, not Christ. If you can't get the big commitment, go for a lesser commitment. I had shared the Gospel with Larry and had used a pocket-sized picture of Christ knocking at the door to explain Revelation 3:20. He was not ready to pray to accept Christ. I asked him to promise me he would think about it and gave him the picture of Christ knocking. I wrote on the back of it and assured Larry I would complete the statement when he opened the door to Christ. That was late Wednesday. Larry put the picture of Christ on the mirror in the bathroom. Every time he shaved, Jesus knocked. On Friday he was in the hardware store purchasing hardware for his kitchen cabinets. The Holy Spirit spoke to him: "You're buying something that will rust. I want to give you something that will last forever." He went out to his car, his objections melted, he prayed, and the Lord Jesus Christ became Larry's Savior. Today he is a member of his local church, Sunday school superintendent, and a man of God!

Discussion Questions

1. What does Ephesians 6:12 teach us about the real enemy, when we face objections?

2. How can objections be seen as opportunities rather than as obstacles?

3. If you had the choice of making a visit to three different people, which of the following would you visit: someone you consider "not open," someone who appears "open," or someone who is "hungry"?

4. What three ways does James Kennedy suggest for handling objections?

5. Why do people raise objections? What is their motive? Who in your group can recall the reason(s) he or she raised objections prior to conversion?

6. How can you give a correct answer to an objection but lose your prospect in the process?

7. Do those who appear to be unreceptive turn out, at times, to be receptive to you and vice versa? How has God surprised you in this regard? *See* John 3:8.

8. How might it help to meet an objection with the question, "Why do you want to know?" *See* Shaver's discussion of John 4 and the following chapter by Moishe Rosen.

10
The Art of Witnessing to the Antagonist (or to the Gospel-Resistant Person)

Moishe Rosen

Some of our more modern technology paints images that help us understand the reality of evangelism and missions. One such term is an insight projected by Ralph Winter, the patriarch of modern missiology. Dr. Winter uses the term *hidden peoples* to refer to primitives tucked away in remote places where they are unseen by the rest of the world.

These might be bush people in Africa or river people in the Amazon basin. Generally speaking, the "hidden people" have no Bible in their own language or contact with concerned Christians who could communicate Christ to them.

Building on Dr. Winter's teaching, I would like to offer another term for understanding a different segment of the world. The term I offer is *hiding people.* It refers to those who deliberately make themselves remote. They live among Christians or have contact with Christians, but they do not want to be reached with the Gospel. When anyone or anything associated with the Bible approaches them, they go into hiding. Most often, they hide behind their own religious precepts, i.e., Judaism, Islam, Buddhism, Hinduism, etc. Sometimes they hide behind one of the many humanistic philosophies.

Yet God did not exclude them from His love or exempt us from our duty to proclaim Christ to them, though at times this might present great difficulty. Often those very people become the most useful to the cause of Christ after their conversion.

When we talk about a people or peoples who resist the Gospel, the Christian must understand that these are good people and, for the most part, moral people. Yet they have been conditioned by their own society to hold certain values.

Many Buddhists are willing to place a statue of Jesus on their godshelf, pray to Him occasionally, and celebrate Christian feasts—as long as they are not called upon to worship Jesus only, or to regard the Bible as the only Holy Book, or separate from a pagan society. They might like the idea of having a little bit of Jesus, but they don't like the formula "Jesus + any other religion = no salvation, no Christianity."

The God of the Bible is a jealous God and will not tolerate being placed with other gods. When this truth is told to a Buddhist, it often results in resistance to the "narrow-minded exclusivism" of the Christian religion.

In most Buddhist countries, the would-be convert to Christianity must reject the common practices and folk philosophies of his own people. If he allows himself to believe that Christianity might be true, it will bring him into conflict with all others.

On the other hand, the Islamic religion inculcates a different reason for being resistant to the Gospel. Like Buddhism, it embraces all of life—the social and governmental institutions, as well. Not only is there the barrier of rejecting one's society but Islam also is an exclusive religion. Jesus will be allowed to be *a* prophet, but Mohammed must be *chief* prophet.

People who are committed to following such a religion also have a commitment not to consider the claims of Christ. Hence, they belong to a social structure that resists the Gospel message for themselves, even though they might tolerate it for Christians.

The Gospel-resistant person reacts to the Gospel before he ever responds. That reaction to the proclamation of the Good News is a searing pain. The person in the Gospel-resistant society hears our proclamation and suddenly realizes that if he listens he might be persuaded. If he's persuaded, he might believe; and if he believes, then he will become an outcast. In that moment he feels a pang. A spiritual shudder rises within him, and he responds, "No! I don't want to believe. I don't want to know. I don't want to be rejected." Then he deflects the Gospel testimony with a joke of some sort or attributes his resistance to some other cause.

On the day of Pentecost, when the crowd heard the wonderful works of God preached in their own languages, those who merely reacted said, "These people are drunk" (Acts 2:13 TEV). But others did not only react. They responded and asked a reasonable question that needed to be answered: "How can they be drunk, since this is only about the third hour of the day? Yet we're hearing these languages by people who never learned them." The responder draws closer while the reactor recoils, but most likely we see the reaction before we see the response. In the Acts 2 account, the hearers reacted reflexively because they knew it had already been decided that any Jew who confessed Christ would be put out of the synagogue (John 9:22).

For those who belong to groups such as Islam, Judaism, Buddhism, etc., resistance to conversion is a *moral* matter. That is to say, a moral person must resist in order to be loyal to his or her own.

Though it is strange to think of Christianity as a kind of immorality, we must remember that religious truth is absolute and not relative. Morality is more concerned with the folkways of a certain group than with revealed truth. Hence, to contemplate those things which might lead to Christian conversion might pose a moral temptation to certain non-Christians. But, like many people who make a token show of denial toward what they consider immoral, it is only a token resistance. Once the *words* of resistance have been spoken, the duty to resist has been met. Then, if the witnessing Christian has not been put off, the witness can proceed.

One of the greatest obstacles to evangelism is the church's vision and image of itself. Pastors are trained in a certain way. Except for lectures in systematic theology or dogmatics, they learn little about how to state a case persuasively. Ministers are trained to preach to and teach the flock, which is composed of those who are already approving and accepting of what is being said.

When pastors are confronted by objections from Gospel-resistant people that they are not trained to meet, it is far easier either to give the objector a book on apologetics that shows the case for Christianity or, worse yet, just to give up and go on to the next person who will receive the message. Often even informed pastors do not learn how to speak to a Gospel-resistant person. For example, what often seems like a question is not intended to evoke knowledge at all. Instead, it is a question the asker knows will confound the Christian. The lack of a suitable answer then serves to uphold the questioner in his or her unbelief.

A good example of this is the way some Jewish people and some Muslims choose to resist the idea of the Trinity. The question might go like this: "How can any man become God?" The very way the question is asked shows resistance. The questioner knows full well that if there is a God, no man can ever become God, because virtually all religions define God as being eternally existent. So the first thing we see is that the challenger is asking the wrong question, since one must either agree or prove that man can become God.

That question ignores the biblical assumption that God became man in the Incarnation. You might think such a questioner is merely confused, but as often as not, that person is not confused. Rather he is determined to confound you, the evangelist, and thus reassure himself of the superiority of his own position. Perhaps such a question should not even be answered and the asker should not be dealt with at that point. In any case, we must be very careful not to give the right answer to the wrong question.

Most Christians would typically and erroneously answer the above question by quoting Scriptures that prophesy the Incarnation. Yet the way to begin is with thought-provoking questions of your own: "Why do you ask?" "Why do you want to know?" "In what way would my answer advance your knowledge?" (We will provide more leading questions later.) In other words, the best way is to catch the challenger off guard. Most pastors, however, are not prepared to do that.

The pastor is taught to minister to those who have submitted to his spiritual authority. Thus, he cannot easily deal with those who challenge his message or teaching.

As often as not, a pastor has been taught to regard his church as a parish. Perhaps in the days when people walked to church or drove there in a horse and buggy, that would have been proper, but now it's not unusual for a parishioner to drive thirty minutes and pass five churches of like faith to settle into one church. Locality has little to do with parish identification. It's not a matter of geography but a matter of communication.

A pastor should think of his parish as *those who are willing to listen to him,* whether or not they become communicants of his church. The fact that people live in convenient proximity to his house of worship hardly places them in his parish. They are reachable to that pastor only if they will allow him to communicate God's message to them.

Furthermore, many different kinds of people from various cultures may live in one geographic location. A pastor from one specific culture will probably have difficulty communicating to those who are not of that culture or who hold no particular respect for clergy.

Some might say that the modern concept of church planting is backwards. A group or denomination sends a pastor to build a church, hoping to attract worshipers. This might or might not happen, but announcing a meeting is not enough. Ministers are not like other professionals who can hang out a shingle and hope for the patronage of the community.

The establishment of a formal congregation should be secondary to winning people to Christ. When we take the Person of Christ to the people, we understand the verity of His statement, "But I, when I am lifted up from the earth, will draw all men to myself" (John 12:32).

The church can no longer count on a Christianized culture to represent it. Our culture through its accepted agencies, i.e., television, radio, and newspapers, points people to the movie theaters, the discount stores, and the products that pay to be touted. Even televised religious programs do not primarily point people to any church. Though our culture is thought to be Christianized, for the most part it is indifferent, even hostile, to the Gospel message.

Hence, the establishment of a congregation before there is a community of faith strikes a Jewish person like me as absurd. In Jewish thought, wherever ten Jewish males are gathered together, that is a viable congregation by virtue of their Jewishness.

We who would evangelize the lost need to begin reaching a Gospel-resistant culture by gaining a new vision of what God wants the church to become and how it should function. Compare the early church of Acts 2 to the church of today. Where was the church? What was its parish? What did they do differently?

When the church was still largely Jewish, the faithful were not so concerned about location. The Jews were always a highly mobile people in the diaspora. They could meet in someone's home or in a cave. As long as the temple stood, the apostles at Jerusalem worshiped there over the objection of other Jews who did not want to be infected by the virus of the messianic faith. They did not establish a parish system. Rather, they recognized that the church was centered around the Person of Christ. They did not need a myriad of rules and regulations about who was going to pay for what and what would be allowed or forbidden. They had only one rule, and that rule was love.

The early church so loved the Lord Jesus Christ and reflected that love to one another that John could say their testimony to the world would be, "All men will know that you are my disciples, if you love one another" (John 13:35). They were ready to say, "What is mine is yours," without requiring the other to respond, "And what's mine is yours, also." They were not so concerned with getting and having as they were with confessing and giving, and all the people shared what they had.

They met every day, not merely one day a week, for worship. Instruction in apostolic times was a "learn as you go" sort of experience. Communion was held at virtually every meal. Jesus ordained apostles, and the apostles ordained others, but they did not seek to stabilize into parishes. Location was almost incidental. Wherever the believers were, they were bound together as the church.

It was all so simple. Those who knew, taught. Those who had, shared. Those who needed, received. The early church had no concept of church planting or missions because they never saw the church as fixing itself in a location. The church that is static can reach only its own.

When the church does try to interface with others who belong to Gospel-resistant communities, too often it uses a standard method of dealing with them. The church treats those non-Christian resisters as if they wanted to know the Gospel and their resistance was simply based on a misunderstanding. The church wrongly thinks that if it could only help those resistant outsiders understand the Gospel message, they would want to believe it.

Some say that dialogue is the way to win over the resisters, but dialogue means more than listening to the other person until it's your time to talk. The greatest problem with dialogue is that it lowers Christianity, the Gospel, and the person of Christ to the level of negotiation. Our faith is presented as no more than our tradition, our teaching, or our opinion.

If Christ is merely the main character in our religious tradition and He has no more reality outside of our existence, then the resurrection didn't really happen and, as the Apostle Paul says, "We are to be pitied more than all men" (1 Corinthians 15:19). We cannot lower the person of Christ and package Him to be presented as our teaching or our tradition.

Real dialogue is not a possibility. Hence, what passes for dialogue is not dialogue at all but a structured situation where we listen with a view toward learning the other person's feelings and seeking to find an opening to present the Gospel.

Such a pretense is not really honest. The true Christian is not open-minded to hear why or how another religion might be true. He is only open-minded to discover how he might proclaim Christ to others. This sounds narrow-minded, and indeed it is. Nevertheless, one can believe in absolute truth, believe that faith to be absolutely well placed, and still be tolerant, loving, thoughtful, sympathetic, and helpful to others who do not believe the same things.

In Christ we are enabled to love those who are otherwise unlovable and to uphold those who cannot lift themselves. The Gospel is not merely truth that is waiting to be discovered. It is the interactive *power* of God unto salvation. We can be as loving as Jesus was to the woman at the well. (He never told her that her life-style was right.) We can be as loving as He was to the rich young ruler or to the Syro-Phoenician woman. We should uncompromisingly declare what is true and what is right and then love those who cannot comprehend it.

This does not mean we can be arrogant or even declare that we are right. Rather, we declare that *Christ* is right. It is not that *we* are truthful but that *He* is truth. It is not that *our* way leads to God but that *His* way leads to God. We do not proclaim ourselves but the One who is far better than we could ever become.

Special Communication Techniques

Some of the techniques we use in Jewish evangelism to persuade Gospel-resistant people may seem a bit strange to those who belong to a Christian or Gentile culture. But one thing that is very effective with Jewish people is this question: "What do you think God wants you to do?" Some will say, "He wants me to be a good person," or "He wants me to follow the law," or "He wants [this or that]." Once in a while someone will shrug and say, "Who knows?" To this we answer, "You *can* know." But whatever they say positively, I answer, "So, then, why don't you do it?"

With Jews, it's easy to move from law to grace. Another technique that is effective in getting the person to accept the first premise is, "If the Bible is true and Jesus is the Messiah, are you willing to find out and believe, even though it might have severe social consequences?" Christians are constantly surprised by how many Jewish people answer no to that question. "No" is not necessarily a bad answer. I know from personal experience. Before I became a believer, when I realized I had said no because I didn't want to find out, it helped me see that I had turned my back on possible truth, and that for the first time in my life I had really avoided a question.

At such a point in talking to a resister, conversational techniques became very important. Here are some techniques we have found effective in Jewish evangelism when the person said, "No, I'm not interested":

1. *Provide a defense that is unacceptable to the person.* Give people defenses against your position. Help them along. Make excuses for them. Say something like, "Yes, you're right. I can understand why you wouldn't want to know. After all, you're not really a scholar. You couldn't be expected to know things like that." Or say, "I can understand why you don't want to know. You would feel it wrong to go against the thinking of your crowd." Or indicate that, "of course, you would never want to deviate from the crowd." (Intimate that they are just one of the flock, one of the cattle who goes along with the intellectual stampede.)

In other words, provide them with excuses that are unconscionable to them. You might say, "I can understand why you wouldn't want to hear something like this. After all, if you believed what I believe, you might have to do some things you didn't want to do." Provide them with excuses that are unacceptable. To reject those excuses they will have to open the windows of their minds for a moment.

2. *Use the salesman's ploy.* There is a book titled something like *The Sale Begins When the Customer Says No.* The author of that book is not lying. If a person tells you no and says he's not interested, that's when you know you have a real opportunity and a challenge. Being ignored is worse than getting a negative reaction. You can interact with a negative reaction, but you cannot interact with silence.

Here's what a salesman might say in response to a negative answer: "I know you are not going to buy my product, but help me to understand so I can do it right the next time. Explain to me why this product is not usable by a knowledgeable person like yourself. I can tell you really want a ———, and I need to know why my presentation of it doesn't meet your needs. Just take a couple of minutes and help me."

That's the salesman's ploy, but here is how it translates into a witnessing tool: You can say, "I know you don't want to hear what I have to say about Jesus, but could you help me understand why an open-minded, articulate person like you feels ill at ease discussing it? Help me do it right."

There is a second, important part to this. When the person does tell you why he or she doesn't want to discuss it, don't use that admission as a tool to begin leveraging the person into discussing it, as the salesman would. Simply say, "Oh, I see. Thank you. You've helped me understand." That gives you the ability to come back another time and say, "I thought about what you said in our last conversation. It was very instructive to me. Do you mind if I ask you two or three more questions?"

In other words, allow for a break. Just say, "Oh, I see. Thank you very much." Then come back at them later with two or three other questions, no matter what they have told you.

Another conversation technique employs the use of leading questions. Leading questions are so named because they go somewhere. (Remember, the person has already said no.)

> *Leading Question #1*
> "I know you are not going to let me talk to you, but if you did, what do you think I would say? In other words, you have some idea of what I am going to say to which you are saying no. I'd like to find out what it is."

> *Leading Question #2*
> "If the people in your circle of friends ever talk about

Jesus, who do they say He is? If you don't want to hear about Him, evidently you have heard some pretty rotten things about Him."

Leading Question #3
"I know you don't want to talk about Jesus, but do you mind if I talk it over with your father? Your mother? Your religious leader? Some scholar? Let me tell you what I want to tell your mother. How do you think she'd feel about it if I told her God loved her and had a wonderful plan for her life?"

Leading Question #4
"Can I ask you something? I know you don't want to hear about Jesus, but if all the Jewish people in the world suddenly began to believe in Jesus, would you go along with them?"

Leading Question #5
"So the way I understand it, you think the Bible is trash, like last week's newspaper, right?" This question is like giving an unacceptable defense. It's a quality statement of putting words in a person's mouth that will make him uncomfortable.

In Addition to Witnessing and Winning

As important as it is to know how to witness to Gospel-resistant people, it is just as important to know how to nurture those from such a group who do respond to the Gospel. When people come from a culture that would cast them out for converting, the evangelist and the Christian community must make extraordinary efforts to do the following:

1. *Provide a nurturing home.* It's not enough to put someone up in a boarding house, the YMCA, or some such residence. You must be prepared to take in the new

convert, provide succor and spiritual nurture and encourage growth.

2. *Teach the converts how to tell the members of their family about their conversion.* They should begin one at a time with the most accepting and sympathetic family member, who then might urge the others to moderation. But it is important for them to tell the family before they are baptized, lest the family feel betrayed.

3. *Teach the converts to avoid countermissionaries.* In virtually every Gospel-resistant group that interfaces with missionaries and evangelists, there will be some anti-Christian or antimissionary league. The family often asks the potential convert to meet one of these special scholars who knows about such things. The convert *should not meet* with that person or persons.

The basic technique the countermissionary uses is to try to confound the convert by asking questions the convert cannot answer. This is intended to lead converts to the conclusion that since they do not know everything and cannot answer all possible questions, they should defer being baptized until they have properly studied the matter. That's the first line of defense.

The second line of defense is to demonstrate the cruel, uncivilized nature of Christians and thus confuse the converts into thinking they have been deceived. But even though a person might be of such strong character as to resist countermissionaries, there is another danger: the parents and the family of the convert put great stock in the special scholar. Actually, they're grasping at straws. But when the countermissionary fails to deconvert the family member, he then blames it on the contrariness of the convert and urges the family to keep up their pressure of disapproval. He might even convince the family that they have not shown enough disapproval to make the convert realize the consequences of his or her actions and attitude.

Hence, after seeing these specialists, usually the convert sees an even more hardened attitude in the family.

The church among Gospel-resistant people must be able to provide much more than worship, instruction, and fellowship. It must be the society for the convert who has been made an outcast. It must be ready to provide those things that previously had been provided by the Gospel-resistant society. The church must be so much more in those circumstances.

In Conclusion

Some Christians will look at resistant communities and say, "Let's reach the easily reachable first." The Apostle Paul looked at the most Gospel-resistant community of his day. He told the Roman church, which was possibly the only entirely non-Jewish church, "I am not ashamed of the gospel, because it is the power of God for the salvation of everyone who believes: first for the Jew, then for the Gentile" (Romans 1:16).

The Apostle Paul knew something about the difficulties of the ministry. He knew that if you start with the difficult task first and spend much of your creative and spiritual energy communicating to the difficult people, the task is accomplished faster. Human nature makes us want to avoid those who are difficult and begin with those who are easy. We often confuse the difficult with the impossible, but when it comes to evangelism, no person, no people, no place is impossible for the Holy Spirit to penetrate.

One thing the believer must remember is that by nature—human nature—people don't want to be saved from their sins. It is normal, natural, and all too human to love our sins. Not only that, the human heart will deceive us into thinking that any condition which allows us to do what we want must certainly be right.

There is the fear that by using wrong techniques, being insensitive, or giving an improper explanation, we are turning people off. The fact is that you cannot turn *off* a person who has never been turned *on*. If the Holy Spirit is turning someone on, nothing can turn him off. God is invincible and is not defeated.

We must remember that it is neither our battle nor our war. It will not be settled by those who are mighty among men. We do well to continually remind ourselves, " 'Not by might nor by power, but by my Spirit,' says the Lord Almighty" (Zechariah 4:6). If it is truly the might of the Holy Spirit, then we must muster our energies toward the task of prayer and toward the task of pushing ahead at the impulse of the Holy Spirit. We know that as we sow Gospel seed, even on difficult ground, there will be a harvest, and we must place ourselves in the position of being sowers as well as reapers in the more difficult fields of evangelism.

Discussion Questions

1. In what sense are all people resistant to the Gospel? *See,* for example, Ephesians 2:1–3.

2. How are the people discussed in this chapter resistant in a unique way?

3. Are all questions from non-Christians questions for information? For what other reasons do they raise questions before Christians?

4. What is the wisdom of the question, "Why do you want to know?"

5. Do you sometimes treat non-Christians as though

misunderstanding were the only problem, as though the simple understanding of the Gospel would result in faith? Why is that at times incorrect? *See* 1 Corinthians 2:14.

6. How did it help Moishe Rosen to be asked, "If the Bible is true and Jesus is the Messiah, are you willing to find out and believe, even though it might have severe social consequences?"

7. What value do leading questions have in witnessing? Are there potential pitfalls?

8. Discuss the potential of the second leading question: "If the people in your circle of friends ever talk about Jesus, who do they say He is? If you don't want to hear about Him, evidently you have heard some pretty rotten things about Him." You may wish to discuss each leading question.

9. Why should a convert tell the family before being baptized? What does Rosen say? Are there any other reasons?

10. Are you willing to become the society for the convert who has been made an outcast, if that is necessary?

11. React to this statement by Moishe Rosen: "There is the fear that by using wrong techniques, being insensitive, or giving an improper explanation, we are turning people off. The fact is that you cannot turn *off* a person who has never been turned *on*." Do you agree? Why or why not?

11
The Art of Witnessing to the Apathetic

Win Arn and Charles Arn

Why even bother witnessing to the apathetic? They are not receptive. Your witness would probably not even be heard. Until people are receptive, not much is accomplished . . . and apathetic people are resistant.

A true story was told to me at a church growth seminar by Randy, a Presbyterian pastor. It was of special interest because it involved my son-in-law, now also a Presbyterian pastor.

The setting was the University of Washington, where both of these young men were then students living in the same fraternity house. My son-in-law, Joe Bettridge, had recently become a Christian. Shortly thereafter, Randy came to Joe, and in a rather apathetic and unconcerned way, asked Joe what had happened to him. Joe smiled and said, "You wouldn't understand," and walked away. This answer made Randy a little more interested in Joe's new behavior.

Being around him during the next few weeks, Randy began to take more notice of a changed person. He again asked Joe what had happened to him, to which Joe responded, "Have you ever heard of Jesus Christ?"

"Yeah," Randy answered, "like Easter and Christmas." Again Joe turned and walked away with the words, "See, I told you that you wouldn't understand."

Randy was becoming increasingly interested in what had made the difference in Joe. A few weeks later, Randy could be put off no longer. He again approached Joe. Standing in the doorway, he said, "I'm not going to let you out of this room until you tell me what happened to you, Joe." Whereupon Joe proceeded to present the claims of Christ, and Randy, too, became a Christian. As mentioned earlier, today they are both Presbyterian pastors.

What had happened during those intervening weeks?

Randy had moved from apathy to interest to receptivity. The results change dramatically and positively when people move from apathy to receptivity.

Dr. Donald McGavran, founder of the modern Church Growth Movement and former thirty-year missionary to India, observed a remarkable phenomenon years ago on the mission field. He noted that when the Gospel was presented, in some instances the message was readily accepted. In other villages, the same message was presented, but no one responded. His conclusion was that when entire villages or groups of people came to faith in a short period of time, it was because they were receptive. Those who did not were resistant.

Dr. McGavran also observed that some tribes and castes of people tended to move from resistance to receptivity while other groups were moving from receptivity to resistance. His subsequent recommendation to missionaries who desired to see the Christian harvest in greater numbers, was to seek out receptive people groups—people whom God had prepared—and focus evangelistic strategy on the persons in these groups.

Toward that end, Dr. McGavran developed what he called a "receptivity/resistance axis." He contended that people—and even "people groups"—could be placed somewhere on this receptivity/resistance axis. He also contended that people and "people groups" were constantly moving back and forth on this scale.

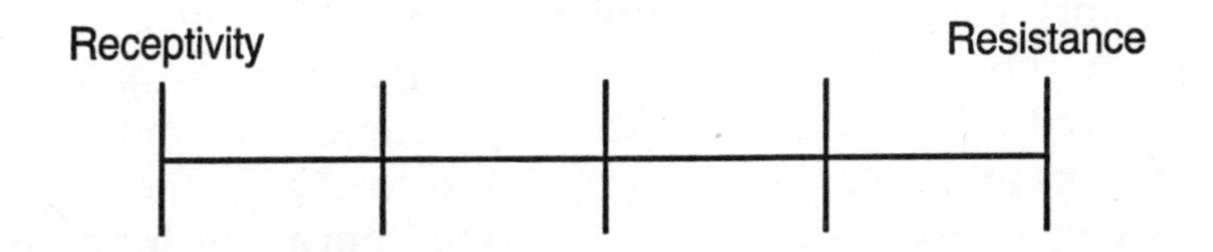

This fact of receptivity/resistance has also been observed by every thinking pastor who has recognized that people, at certain times in their lives, tend to be more receptive than at other times. For example, at the time of a funeral, a wedding, the birth of a child . . . those involved tend to be more receptive to change in their life-style and relationship to God. What pastor hasn't visited a church member in the hospital, paused to pray for a nonmember/non-Christian in an adjoining bed . . . and found that person very receptive.

So the art of witnessing to the apathetic is to be sensitive when they move from apathy to receptivity.

How does one know when this change occurs?

One of the best guides is the Holmes and Rahe Social Readjustment Rating Scale developed by two physicians at the University of Washington. The two identified various changes in life's situations that people experience and ranked them in severity of intensity of effect. The researchers then examined the relationship between persons experiencing these transitional events and the likelihood of their being hospitalized. They observed a strong correlation: Stressful life events often result in debilitating physical symptoms.

To use the scale, indicate events that have taken place in your life during the past twelve months. Then add the numerical values for the items indicated to come up with your score. If you score below 150 points, you are on the safe side. If you score between 150 and 300 points, you have a fifty-fifty chance of becoming ill or disabled during the next two years. If you score over 300 points, your chances of becoming ill increase to 90 percent.

A subsequent study took this same stress scale and looked for relationships between these life transition events and whether persons tended to change their religious life-style—specifically, moving from an unchurched life-style to Christian faith.[1] Again a strong correlation was found. People tended to become Christian and active church members much more often during times of change.

The graph below shows the results of this study:

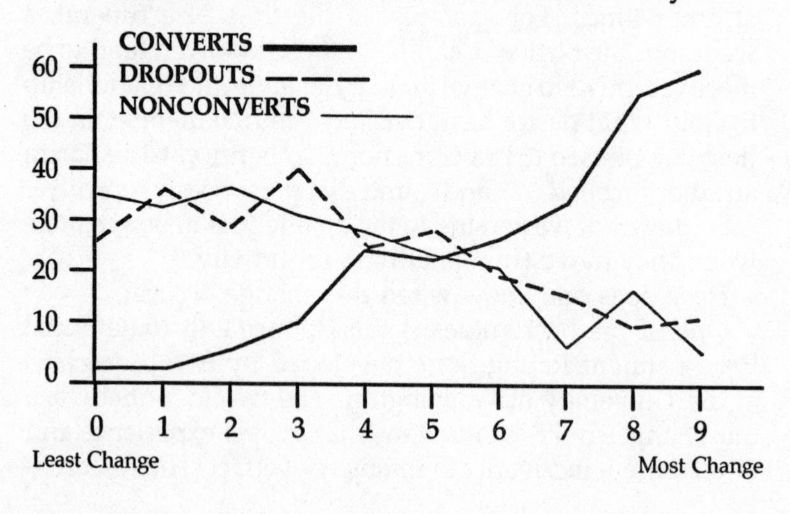

When traditional points of reference were changed, people seemed to be open to other changes in their lives.

In the *Institute for American Church Growth* magazine, we presented the original adult scale, plus four other adaptations of this stress scale, from preschool through high school. These scales are reprinted below. In addition, we have developed a senior adult scale, highlighting transitional events, their relative effect on people's lives, and the receptivity level created to the Gospel at these particular times.

In each of these people groups, the identified events provide windows of opportunity in which people seem to move from apathy or indifference to the Gospel to receptivity and openness. Another way of seeing these events is as experiences the Holy Spirit uses to open people's eyes to needs that cannot be filled in human terms.

Preschool Age

Life Event	*Rank*
Death of a parent	89
Divorce of parents	78
Marital separation of parents	74
Jail sentence of a parent for one year or more	67
Marriage of a parent to a stepparent	62
Serious illness requiring hospitalization	59
Death of a brother or sister	59
Acquiring visible deformity	52
Serious illness requiring hospitalization of a parent	51
Birth of a brother or sister	50
Mother taking job	47
Increase in arguments between parents	44
Starting nursery school	42

Addition of a third adult to family (e.g., grandparent)	39
Brother or sister leaving home	39
Having visible congenital deformity	39
Increase in number of arguments with parents	39
Change in acceptance by peers	38
Death of a close friend	38
Serious illness requiring hospitalization of brother or sister	37
Change in father's job requiring increased absence from home	36
Jail sentence of a parent for 30 days or less	34
Discovery of being adopted	33
Change to new nursery school	33
Death of a grandparent	30
Outstanding personal achievement	23
Loss of job by parent	23
Decrease in number of arguments with parents	22
Decrease in number of arguments between parents	21
Change in parents' financial status	21

Elementary School Age

Life Event	*Rank*
Death of a parent	91
Divorce of parents	84
Marital separation of parents	78
Acquiring a physical deformity	69
Death of a brother or sister	68
Jail sentence of parent for one year or more	67
Marriage of parent to stepparent	65
Serious illness requiring hospitalization	62
Becoming involved with drugs or alcohol	61
Having a visible congenital deformity	60
Failure of a grade in school	57

Serious illness requiring hospitalization of parent	55
Death of a close friend	53
Discovery of being an adopted child	52
Increase in number of arguments between parents	51
Change in child's acceptance by peers	51
Birth of a brother or sister	50
Increase in number of arguments with parents	47
Move to a new school district	46
Beginning school	46
Suspension from school	46
Change in father's occupation requiring increased absence from home	45
Mother beginning to work	44
Jail sentence of parent for 30 days or less	44
Serious illness requiring hospitalization of brother or sister	41
Addition of third adult in family (e.g., grandparent)	41
Outstanding personal achievement	39
Loss of job by parent	38
Death of a grandparent	36
Brother or sister leaving home	36
Pregnancy in unwed teenage sister	36
Change in parents' financial status	29
Beginning another school year	27
Decrease in number of arguments with parents	27
Decrease in number of arguments between parents	25
Becoming a full-fledged member of a church	25

Junior High Age

Life Event	*Rank*
Pregnancy out of wedlock	95
Death of a parent	94
Divorce of parents	84
Acquiring a visible deformity	83

Marital separation of parents	77
Jail sentence of a parent for one year or more	76
Male partner in pregnancy out of wedlock	76
Death of a brother or sister	71
Having a visible congenital deformity	70
Discovery of being an adopted child	70
Becoming involved with drugs or alcohol	70
Change in child's acceptance by peers	68
Death of close friend	65
Marriage of a parent to stepparent	63
Failure of a grade in school	62
Pregnancy in unwed teenage sister	60
Serious illness requiring hospitalization	57
Beginning to date	55
Suspension from school	54
Serious illness requiring hospitalization of a parent	54
Move to a new school district	52
Jail sentence of a parent for 30 days or less	50
Birth of a brother or sister	50
Failure to be accepted in an extracurricular activity he/she wanted	48
Loss of job by a parent	48
Increase in number of arguments between parents	48
Breaking up with boyfriend or girlfriend	47
Increase in number of arguments with parents	46
Beginning junior high school	45
Outstanding personal achievement	45
Serious illness requiring hospitalization of brother or sister	44
Change in father's occupation requiring increased absence from home	42
Change in parents' financial status	40
Mother beginning to work	36
Death of a grandparent	35
Addition of a third adult to family (e.g., grandparent)	34

Brother or sister leaving home	33
Decrease in number of arguments between parents	29
Decrease in number of arguments with parents	29
Becoming a full-fledged member of a church	28

Senior High School Age

Life Event	*Rank*
Getting married	101
Unwed pregnancy	92
Death of a parent	87
Acquiring a visible deformity	81
Divorce of parents	77
Male partner in pregnancy out of wedlock	77
Becoming involved with drugs or alcohol	76
Jail sentence of a parent for one year or more	75
Marital separation of parents	69
Death of a brother or sister	68
Change in acceptance by peers	67
Pregnancy in unwed teenage sister	64
Discovery of being an adopted child	64
Marriage of a parent to stepparent	63
Death of a close friend	63
Having a visible congenital deformity	62
Serious illness requiring hospitalization	58
Failure of grade in school	56
Move to a new school district	56
Failure to be accepted in an extracurricular activity he/she wanted	55
Serious illness requiring hospitalization of a parent	55
Jail sentence of a parent for 30 days or less	53
Breaking up with a boyfriend or girlfriend	53
Beginning to date	51
Suspension from school	50

Birth of a brother or sister	47
Increase in number of arguments with parents	46
Increase in number of arguments between parents	46
Loss of job by a parent	46
Outstanding personal achievement	46
Change in parents' financial status	45
Being accepted at a college of his/her choice	43
Beginning senior high school	42
Serious illness requiring hospitalization of brother or sister	41
Change of father's occupation requiring increased absence from home	38
Brother or sister leaving home	37
Death of a grandparent	36
Addition of third adult to family (e.g., grandparent)	34
Becoming a full-fledged member of a church	31
Decrease in number of arguments between parents	28
Decrease in number of arguments with parents	26
Mother beginning to work	26

Adult

Life Event	*Rank*
Death of a spouse	100
Divorce	73
Marital Separation	65
Jail term	63
Death of a close family member	63
Personal injury or illness	53
Marriage	50
Fired from work	47
Marital reconciliation	45
Change of health of family member	44
Pregnancy	40

Sexual difficulties	39
Addition to family	39
Business readjustment	39
Change in financial status	38
Death of a close friend	37
Change in number of marital arguments	35
Mortgage over $50,000	31
Foreclosure of mortgage or loan	30
Change in work responsibilities	29
Son or daughter leaving home	29
Trouble with in-laws	29
Outstanding personal achievement	28
Spouse starts work	26
Change in living conditions	25
Revision of personal habits	24
Trouble with the boss	23
Change in work hours/conditions	20
Change in residence	20
Change in social activities	18
Mortgage or loan less than $50,000	17
Easter season	17
Change in sleeping habits	16
Change in number of family gatherings	15
Vacation	13
Christmas	12
Minor law violation	11

Arn Modified Senior Stress Scale

Adult Age Life Event	*Rank*
Death of a spouse	100
Divorce	73
Move to retirement home	70
Marital separation	65

Death of a close family member	63
Major physical problems	53
Remarriage	50
Christmas following loss of spouse	49
Realization of no meaningful faith for eternity	47
Financial loss of retirement money	47
Forced early retirement	46
Unable to maintain driver's license	45
Marital reconciliation	45
Retirement	45
Spouse confined to retirement home	45
Change in health of family member	44
Grandchild marries	39
Change in financial status	38
Death of a close friend	37
Difficulty getting medical insurance	36
Change in number of arguments with spouse	35
Foreclosure of mortgage or loan	30
Feelings of not being needed	29
Feelings of lack of purpose	28
Spouse retires	26
Significantly decreased contact with children	25
Revision of personal habits	24
Significantly decreased contact with the church	24
Significantly decreased contact with grandchildren	23
Minor physical problems	20
Change in recreation habits	19
Change in social activities	18
Change in sleeping habits	16
Change in number of family get-togethers	15
Change in eating habits	15
Minor law violation	11

One of the best ways to show that the Christian faith and your church community provide a relevant response to issues people face is to plan outreach/caring ministries around some of these transitional events. For example, we were recently conducting a seminar in a Lutheran church. Across the hall, at the same time, the church was holding a support-group meeting for those who had suffered a stroke. Over twenty people were in attendance, only several of whom had previously been involved in a church.

A Baptist pastor from Washington recently told us of their Crisis Deployment Team, made up of members who are specially trained in helping persons deal with the loss of a spouse or loved one. All those members involved had personal experience in this transitional event. It has been an effective way for the church to provide tangible expression of Christ's healing love and see many come to faith and church involvement. The pastor also told me that the helping process had serendipitously helped those on the crisis teams to deal with their own sense of loss and grief.

The strategy should be clear for effectively witnessing to the apathetic. Christ modeled it and instructed His followers in it: "Turn your eyes to the fields that are ripe unto harvest" (*see* John 4:35). Find receptivity. If the fields are not "ripe," wait until they are. But don't wait too long. The fields are not ripe forever.

In considering the art of witnessing to the apathetic, here is another fascinating and important insight we have observed: Many times the people we consider apathetic to the Gospel are actually apathetic to the *method* used in transmitting the Gospel, not to the Gospel itself. When the method changes, receptivity is often discovered.

A few years ago, a well-known parachurch organization embarked on a massive, nationwide telephone campaign. They recruited thousands of church members to dial tens of thousands of people and share the Gospel over the telephone. Subsequent studies indicated a discouraging growth rate for participating churches. But in the context of this discussion on receptivity, one of the fascinating observations from our studies was that for six months following that nationwide phone blitz, the field had been "burned over" and any other group that tried a similar approach met with great resistance.

Apathetic and/or resistant people are often resistant to the method rather than the message.

So why do people often see the method for doing evangelism limited to only one technique?

It is strange but true that people usually assume the way they personally came to faith in Jesus Christ is the way everyone does (or should). Therefore, the method they experienced is the best method of evangelism.

In reality, there are hundreds of methods of communicating the Good News—some methods more likely to be effective with certain people than others. Therefore, the effective witness is familiar with a *variety of methods* and approaches and endeavors to identify the most appropriate method for the particular case at hand.

In conclusion, here are a few other brief insights we have found personally helpful in the art of witnessing to the apathetic:

- Build loving relationships with people you are in regular contact with. The Great Commandment, to love, and the Great Commission, to make disciples, are really two sides of one coin. The command "to love" appears more frequently in Scripture than any other command and provides a foundational platform to the art of witnessing to the apathetic.

- Provide many different ways for the apathetic person to hear the Gospel. Research indicates that converts who remain active in the Christian faith and life have heard the Gospel an average of six different times prior to their conversion. In contrast, those who made a profession of faith but are now inactive heard the Gospel an average of twice. How might these exposures occur? Personal testimony, literature, sermons, Bible study, listening to others pray, etc. The more ways a person experiences Christians and their faith, the more likely a lifelong commitment will result.

- Introduce the apathetic person to other Christians who could be his or her friends—Christians with similar interests, ages, family and marital status, or who share common concerns. Friendship is a key factor in effective witnessing.
- Pray regularly for God to move the apathetic person you are concerned with from resistance to receptivity. Be sensitive and ready when God does.

Discussion Questions

1. What insights from chapters 1–9 can you draw on for witnessing to the apathetic?
2. Are apathetic people always apathetic (to the Gospel)? Do you know of anyone who left apathy behind? Do you know why?
3. What reasons do the Arns give for moving away from apathy?
4. Is apathy often a front for what's going on inside? If so, how could this help you approach an apathetic person?

5. Are you apathetic about anything? Can you explain why? What would motivate you to change?

6. After looking at the various adaptations of the Holmes-Rahe Stress Scale for the various age groups, who among your acquaintances might be open?

7. What could your church do now to reach people who have experienced one of the stressful events listed in the Stress Scale?

8. If people can be apathetic about the method rather than the message, could they be apathetic about anything else? For example, could a different messenger get through?

12
The Art of Witnessing Cross-Culturally

Donald McGavran

This book is written for Christians living in America. How can these Christians witness effectively to other Americans of different cultures? Many of these other Americans are their neighbors and friends or live in the same cities.

Large numbers of Japanese, Chinese, Muslims, Hindus, Buddhists, secularists, and humanists from many countries have poured into America and now live in many large cities from Maine to California. How can the Christian witness effectively cross-culturally?

What does *cross-culturally* mean in the United States, where many strands of humanity are gradually becoming one? Their children go to the same schools. They get paid equal amounts for equal work. All have an equal vote.

Nevertheless, Christians in America look out on many other Americans who consider themselves quite different. The 5 or 6 million Jews who live in the United States consider themselves a totally different people. So do the 2 million Muslims, the hundreds of thousands of French Canadians, the Puerto Ricans, Colombians, Mexicans, Filipinos, and on and on. We Americans are one people in a very limited sense. We are in fact many peoples.

Is it true that all Americans have one culture? No, Americans live in many different cultures. American Indians think of themselves as quite different people. So do the quarter million Filipinos now living in California. So do the brown-skinned scholars and businesspeople coming from India, and their children and grandchildren.

Indeed, the tremendous political move to make English the only language in which government documents are written is being seriously challenged by the Hispanic populations, who say, "We don't understand English nearly as well as we do Spanish. Since we want to vote intelligently, write out the directions in Spanish."

This chapter speaks to this wonderful American population, "one nation under God," and at the same time a conglomerate of many different cultures, many different relationships, many different segments of society, all under God. This chapter will speak to how middle-class and upper-middle-class Christians, very largely of European ancestry, will witness effectively to other pieces of the American population. How will white-collar congregations witness in sections of the city where blue-collar people live? How will churches which have grown strong in the German and Scandinavian populations of the north central states witness effectively to the Koreans, Chinese, and Mexicans recently arrived and multiply churches among them? These are the essential questions that members of all branches of the universal church must answer if they would become effective in the art of witnessing cross-culturally.

The Purpose of Witnessing

The purpose of all witnessing about the Lord and Savior Jesus Christ is that men and women may believe on Him as God and only Savior and be saved. The beginning step is witnessing. The end result is that men and women come to believe on Jesus Christ and become part of His body, the church. When they believe, they will not perish but have everlasting life (John 3:16). In short, the purpose of all witnessing is that God's perishing children may be led to believe on the Savior, become practicing Christians, and form Spirit-filled Christian congregations.

This is made perfectly clear in Matthew 28:18, 19. The ultimate Authority in the universe, He to whom "all authority in heaven and on earth has been given" (RSV) clearly states the Great Commission. In Greek this has four verbs—an imperative and three participles. The participles—*going, baptizing,* and *teaching*—explain how the imperative is to be carried out. The imperative is stated in four Greek words, *Matheteusate panta ta ethne.*

I use the Greek words because they have so often been mistranslated. The King James Version says "go . . . and teach all nations." The word *nation* in the year 1610, when the King James Version was first printed, was used for "tribes." When James Fenimore Cooper wrote his famous book *The Last of the Mohicans,* he spoke about "the great Mohican nation." The Mohicans at that time were a small Indian tribe in northern New York State numbering no more than eight thousand men!

The command the Lord actually gave was, *Matheteusate panta ta ethne. Matheteusate* means, "Incorporate in My body the church." *Panta ta ethne* means, "all the pieces of the vast human mosaic"—all the minorities, racial groupings, neighborhoods, and on and on. That is clearly what the ultimate Authority in the universe commands American Christians today to do.

Discipling Within Cultures

Carrying out the Great Commission must not take men and women out of one culture and thrust them into another. The Apostle Paul based his entire ministry on this principle. He insisted that Gentiles could become Christians within their culture, just as the Jews did. They did not have to be circumcised. They did not have to give up bacon and ham, delicious foods. They did not have to cease being Romans or Greeks, Macedonians or Ephesians. God-blessed Christians could be Gentiles as well as Jews.

Americans carrying out the Great Commission must realize that, despite an official trend toward a unified American citizenship, most segments of American society will become Christians while remaining culturally themselves—different from Americans whose ancestors came from northern Europe, Scotland, or Wales.

The Multitudinous Pieces of the Mosaic

The art of discipling *panta ta ethne* demands that all *simplistic* ideas of the "other populations" of the United States be abandoned. Every state in the union is a mosaic of many segments of society.

The mosaic of mankind is abundantly documented in the Bible. The Old Testament is full of references to segments of society: Amorites, Jebusites, Hivites, Philistines, and the twelve tribes of Israel. Furthermore, it speaks about the rich and the poor, the rulers and the ruled, the people who have much and the people who have little or nothing.

The New Testament also is full of references to different

peoples. The New Testament word is *ethne*. This is commonly translated "Gentiles," but it should be translated "Gentile segments of society," "Gentile peoples," or "Gentile tribes and castes, clans, and communities."

The population of our great cities is not a single homogeneous, urban population. It is a mosaic made up of many pieces, speaking different languages, living at different economic levels, having varying degrees of education, belonging to various religions.

Each segment must be approached with suitable adjustments to its culture, income, education, language, and religion.

In California live more than a hundred minorities, each of which considers itself a separate people. Men and women in every one of these minorities must be told, "You can become Christians while remaining firmly a part of your minority—a Christian part of it."

In each piece of the mosaic, congregations must be multiplied. In southern California, there are many localities in which the dominant population is only one of the many minorities: Samoans, American Indians, people from two or three clans in China, other Chinese communities composed of people from other clans. Just west of central Los Angeles is Korea Town. It is two or three miles long and a half mile wide. All the businesses there are Korean businesses. Similar ethnic sections are found in many parts of southern California. Then there are recent arrivals from Mexico, Nicaragua, or Costa Rica.

The task is not to bring into one congregation converts from many different communities, merging them into one new English-speaking American congregation. *The task is to multiply congregations in each piece of the mosaic*. Spanish-speaking immigrants from Puerto Rico must usually, when won to Christ, form Puerto Rican congregations, not merely Hispanic congregations. Immigrants from tiny El Salvador must also have many congregations where the El Salvadoreans feel, "We are now worshiping with our own people, the best people in the world: immigrants from El Salvador."

In short, becoming Christian must seldom mean leaving one's own people, one's own community, one's own segment of society, and joining a church that is simply broadly American, Hispanic, or Chinese.

Probably many of the various pieces of the mosaic will in the next century or two merge into an American society. Some whites today are marrying blacks. Some American Indians are marrying whites. Some Portuguese-speaking immigrants or their children are marrying descendants of German or Irish immigrants. Nevertheless, such a mixing of the different strands of the American population takes place slowly across the decades—indeed, across the generations. There are exceptions, but we must not center attention on the exceptions. We must hold the general practice clearly in mind.

The church planter who slowly establishes a congregation made up of individuals from many pieces of the Hispanic population should then encourage and train converts to become themselves multipliers of house churches *within their own segments of the Spanish-speaking population*.

What Needs to Be Done?

We must evangelize people who speak various languages. Great growth will come only as Christward movements are established in each segment. The task is not to evangelize Hispanics. The task is to multiply churches in each segment of the Hispanic population. Men and women like to go to churches where they sing hymns in their own language, where the sermons are delivered in their own dialect, where fellow Christians are recognized as "our people, speaking the language in which we are so fluent, earning about as much as we do, living at our standard of living."

Lay Christians in America, obeying the Great Commission, speaking only English, should recognize that, as the hundred or more segments of American society are evangelized in their own languages, the beginning will be done by American Christians who speak English. These American Christians may not know the many divisions among the minority they are evangelizing. Consequently, growth of these new churches will be slow. As soon as possible, however, those multiplying churches in any minority, if they would evangelize *effectively*, must multiply churches that fit the population being evangelized. They will win Mexican immigrants in English, but the newly won Mexican Christians will evangelize their comrades in Mexican Spanish, not Argentinian or Costa Rican Spanish. The same is true for immigrants from more than a hundred different lands.

Effective evangelization must be done among followers of many religions. Practicing Christians must also learn the religious beliefs of the men and women in their neighborhood. They should know the secularists, humanists, New Age believers, Jews, Hindus, Muslims, and so on. They can learn about this by practicing the art of friendship, the art of asking questions, the gift of hospitality, and good listening skills, explained elsewhere in this book. They can read books, and they can learn from others who understand a particular religion.

They should also know the nominal or notional Christians in their neighborhoods. These, alas, are also non-Christians who will perish and must be recognized as non-Christians. All practicing Christians need to realize that many who call themselves Christians seldom if ever go to church. While they call themselves Christians, the real god they worship is money, success, influence, sex, or community recognition. The multitudinous religions now spreading in nearly all states of the union present practicing Christians with wonderful opportunities for communicating the Gospel, *provided that men and women are approached on their own religious ground within their own thought forms and convictions*. Dick Innes has dealt with this idea quite extensively in his chapter, so I refer you to that chapter.

When Pentecostal Puerto Rican congregations multiplied in New York City in the 1950s, every Pentecostal worshiper, on entering the church, went up to the pulpit, knelt, crossed himself, and then sat down. This was without question Roman Catholic. But it was uniformly practiced in Protestant Pentecostal churches. The church planters were allowing this single element of Roman Catholic culture in a thoroughly Pentecostal congregation.

Effective evangelization must be done in multitudinous cultures. All Christians intent on obeying the Great Commission must also learn the culture. Culture—all across America—is very greatly influenced by the amount of income an average man or woman has. It is also largely influenced by the section of the world from which the immigrant has recently come. Those who have come from West Germany, let us say, will be different from those who have come from Nigeria or Sri Lanka or the Philippines.

While the differences enumerated above are certainly less in the United States than in many other countries, as a whole these differences nevertheless continue to exist. Branches of the universal church made up exclusively of fourth- or fifth-generation northern Europeans must recognize that if they are to disciple the *ethne*, the pieces of the human mosaic recently arrived from Africa, Asia, and Latin America, they must establish congregations and *new pastor training institutions that fit those sections*. If any branch of the church says, "Oh yes, we will multiply Hispanic churches, but these must be as highly educated as we are, and their pastors can be trained in the same institutions as our pastors," then these branches will experience little church growth. Congregations of immigrants from India who consider themselves of a superior caste, who go back to India to get wives for their sons, are not going to join white Lutheran, Episcopalian, Presbyterian, or Baptist congregations where all the Indian members will have considerable difficulty finding wives for their sons or husbands for their daughters.

The services of worship and the instruction leading to suitable worship will differ for every piece of the mosaic. The differences must be there so that all those who worship will feel utterly at home. They will believe, "We are truly worshiping God *in our own way*. What we are saying and singing and praying and hearing is meaningful to us. It is not some foreign way of doing things. It is our way. This feels very good to us."

In summary, Christians must present the Lord Christ—the way, the truth, and the life, without whom no one comes to the Father—to men and women of other pieces of the American mosaic. The Gospel must be presented in ways that enable people to become Christians without leaving their piece of the mosaic. Congregations must be multiplied in each piece of the mosaic so that people can feel, "While we become Christians, we still remain our people." In the New Testament, we read again and again that Jews became Christians while continuing to eat like Jews, marry like Jews, observe the Sabbath on Saturday, not Sunday, and consider themselves thoroughly Jewish. Gentiles did the same. When Greeks became Christians, they did not cease to be Greeks. When Romans became Christians, they did not cease to be Romans. To be sure, non-Christian elements of any culture will be renounced or modified so that they will be acceptable to the Lord Jesus Christ, but the basic principle remains.

Multiplying Congregations

All cross-cultural evangelization must not just proclaim the Gospel or carry out beautiful, meaningful worship services but must also multiply churches in one or more of the *ethne* surrounding them. This conviction lies at the center of all truly effective evangelism. While this has often been said in the preceding pages, it requires special attention.

Adding members to one's own church is not the answer. True, it is part of the answer. But so much church growth is based on a very pleasing and satisfying preacher, a beautiful church building, a wide estimate that this is a wonderful church. These are all excellent reasons for joining a church, but they produce little multiplication of churches.

In many static or slightly declining denominations, there are some greatly growing congregations. Much of this growth comes from transfers. Those Christians moving to a new city look around for a church that pleases them. "Belonging to this congregation," they say, "will be a step upward for us. We like the members of this congregation."

Such church growth is good, but it does not reach out into new sections of the population and win them to a true, Holy Spirit-filled Christian life.

In short, not only must individuals be won to Christ, not only must individuals join beautiful congregations that have wonderful programs, but segments of the population in which few men and women are Christians must have new congregations multiplied among them as well. Church growth does mean growing better and larger congregations, but it must also mean multiplying new congregrations in those sections of the population where the people are nominal Christians or openly non-Christians.

Such church planting will not be easy, but it can be done and indeed must be done. *The Art of Sharing Your Faith* must mean both causing existing churches to grow and multiplying new vital Spirit-filled congregations in undiscipled segments of the population.

Many Segments in Society

Throughout this chapter we have spoken about the many segments in every nation. This is particularly true in the enormous United States, with very different populations in Hawaii and Maine, Alaska and Florida.

What will multiply congregations in Kansas will probably not multiply congregations in Vermont. What will multiply congregations among the Filipino Americans in Los Angeles will not work among the Cuban multitudes now living in Miami.

What is needed is not helping incoming immigrants to better education, more remuneration, or more recognition in the state. What is needed is for every segment of the population to be effectively evangelized. Thus new congregations of that segment of the population will multiply.

Instead of all existing congregations saying, "Let us reach out and bring into this congregation all the Koreans living within a mile of this congregation or all the French Canadians living around this lake in northern Michigan," we should say, "Let us plant congregations that fit the population we are seeking to disciple."

Let us incorporate in Christ's body congregations that are reviving and enlightening segments of the population filled with very nominal or notional Christians, confessing secularists, or New Age followers.

Middle- and Upper-Class Citizens

Most branches of the universal church in the United States and Canada are today composed of middle- and upper-class men and women. To be sure, there are many exceptions. Some branches of the universal church have in the beginning grown from the lower classes. But in the second, third, and fourth generations, these branches, too, have become middle and upper class.

Becoming Christians will lead men and women of the lower classes to become much more reliable, honest, and hardworking and thus able to rise into the middle or upper classes. Congregations that 150 years ago were made up of slightly literate Americans are now branches in which most of the members are high school or college graduates. Being Christian unquestionably causes populations in America to get better educated, rise in the social scale, earn more money, and become middle- or upper-class citizens. President Lincoln had very little formal education, and his parents were doubtless either illiterate or almost illiterate.

Thirty years ago when I taught in a West Virginia college for nine months, I spoke in churches all up and down the state. In cities and towns the churches I found were Baptist, Methodist, Presbyterian, Episcopal, and the like. But in the mining communities and "runs and hollows," there were very few congregations of these denominations. There the congregations came from the Pentecostals, the Nazarenes, and other *beginning* denominations. Desperately needed today are resolves by the old established denominations, whether Lutheran, Methodist, or Baptist, to reach out and multiply congregations in the underprivileged pieces of the American mosaic. Whether these underprivileged pieces are immigrants who have poured in during the past forty years or slightly educated sections of the older population makes little difference.

To be sure, the churches that are established among these less-privileged sections of the American population will not be led by men who have both college and seminary degrees. They will be pastored by good Christian leaders not far removed from the educational and financial positions of their members.

Allowing such pastors to be ordained does, of course, pose a real problem for most branches of the church. Whether this problem is solved by creating two kinds of pastors—one highly educated and one slightly educated—or in some other way is something that needs to be decided.

When we turn from the middle and upper classes to the lower classes, we find a similar multitude of groupings. For example, the enormous publicity given to the homeless indicates the large number of these citizens. Also inner-city populations are quite different from suburban populations. Highly secularized communities are very different from highly Christian communities. Followers of the New Age movement are quite different from committed Christians. All government, whether at local, state, or national level, assumes that every citizen has equal vote and equal power with every other citizen. From this truth, many Americans leap to the *false* position that in consequence, all citizens are substantially the same kind of people. Whether these are Presbyterian, Assemblies of God, or Lutheran, as they seek to obey the ultimate Authority in the universe and carry out the Great Commission (disciple *all* segments of society), Christians must realize that the people being discipled belong to many different segments of society. Each segment will worship and carry on its ministry in its own way.

Thus many different kinds of congregations, led by different kinds of pastors, having different kinds of worship, listening to different kinds of sermons, are clearly necessary if the peoples of this land are to become substantially Christian. If the huge secular, unbelieving, pagan populations now multiplying in the Western world are to become Christian, many different kinds of church life must be both begun and greatly strengthened. Possibly this will happen as different denominations become prominent in different sections of the population. Possibly all thinking denominations (branches of the universal church) will change their present narrow definitions of *church* and *pastor* to describe pastors of wealthy, educated sections of the population and pastors of poverty-stricken, slightly educated sections.

The battle for equality among all pieces of the American mosaic must not wipe out the certainty that these pieces do exist and that each piece can be reached, discipled, and cared for in a manner that suits the piece. Highly educated branches of the universal church must not feel pressured to adopt worship styles that fit the poor, homeless, and unemployed segments of the population, or vice versa. They must always say, "We look out on a population that exists at many different levels. We will multiply congregations in each level. How we do this is our primary problem. That we do this is God's clear directive to us."

Conclusion

The Christian task to which God calls all branches of the universal church in North America and all other lands is discipling all segments of the population. In America, that means whether we are thinking about secular faculties in state universities or the very nominal parts of the 2 million Portuguese-speaking Roman Catholics now living in the United States or any of the other non-Christian or slightly Christian segments of the population, every branch of the universal church should be planning to multiply congregations in all neighboring pieces of the population now unchurched. We need churches in slum populations, university populations, wealthy populations, poor populations, highly educated populations, almost-illiterate populations, suburban populations, inner-city populations, and so on. *Each kind of population will require a somewhat different kind of pastoring and Bible teaching*. University congregations will certainly want their pastors to be highly educated university graduates. But congregations made up of slightly educated recent arrivals from southern Italy or Indonesia must have pastors whose education fits the congregations they serve.

What we have said about America will be better seen if we recognize that we are talking about a *world* situation. When we look overseas at the great unchurched populations in Japan, China, Bangladesh, Burma, Thailand, India, and Libya, to mention only a few, we realize that the population in each of these countries is a mosaic made up of many pieces. The church will grow at a different rate and in different ways in each piece of the mosaic. Discipling the multitudinous pieces of the mosaic will not destroy the mosaic. When the peasants cultivating a couple of acres of land in some village of Asia, Africa, or Latin America become Christians, they will not become car-driving, forty-thousand-dollars-a-year-earning Americans. Their church life will have to fit them.

Indeed, one may say that in the Third World the only pieces of the vast human mosaic that have become solidly Christian are those where the church life fits the culture, degree of education, language, and social and economic standing of a particular piece of the mosaic. Each Christianized piece of the mosaic earns at one of multitudinous levels. Each eats what its own segment of society eats. Each plays as its segment of society plays. Each thinks and acts as that section of society thinks and acts. The mosaic of mankind is a tremendous reality that all those seeking to disciple *panta ta ethne* must recognize. They must incorporate this reality in their plans to propagate the Gospel.

To be avoided at all costs is the conviction that as people become Christians, they become like us. Culturally, linguistically, and financially they will remain entirely themselves. They will continue to earn what they have been earning. They will continue to eat what they have been eating. They will continue to marry young men and young women like themselves. The only elements of their culture they will give up are the sinful ones that are specifically denounced in the Bible. They will be led by pastors whose style of life fits the congregations being established.

The art of discipling cross-culturally will certainly lead to a tremendous multiplication of groups of men and women who believe on the Lord Jesus, read or listen to His Word regularly, and begin to multiply cells of believing, obeying men and women.

Unfortunately, most Christian populations today in practically every land seldom practice the art of discipling God's lost sons and daughters. That has been left to missionaries, ministers, and an occasional ardent evangelist. In sharp contrast to this present widespread situation, in every congregation there must soon arise groups of men and women who strongly believe they cannot be genuine Christians without *themselves* bringing unbelievers to joyous Christian faith. This is the art of discipling. This art will become—indeed, it must become—in the years and decades ahead one of the outstanding characteristics of all branches of the universal church. God will be greatly pleased as this art becomes common practice among all Christians.

Winning the world for Christ is not the task of missionaries only. It is the task of every practicing Christian. The art of discipling *panta ta ethne* rests not on the preacher, minister, and missionaries alone. It also rests on every Christian. An essential duty of every Christian is to lead others to Christian faith. Every Christian should recognize which friend is a believing, practicing Christian and which friend is in reality a secularist, sometimes in Christian clothing. True, some Christians will be more effective than others. Not every Christian can become an effective evangelist. Each Christian, however, can and ought to pray, speak, and work that the lost be found, that those helplessly floating down the river to Niagara Falls are rescued. Every Christian should be consciously aware of the unchurched communities within twenty miles of where he or she lives and do something to disciple the multitudinous non-Christian men and women. These live in every piece of the mosaic surrounding Christian churches.

Indeed, God would gently remind us that discipling is the heart of His command. He does not vaguely wish this to happen. He commands His followers to do it and gives them power to obey His command.

Discussion Questions

1. What principles from the first nine chapters apply to sharing your faith cross-culturally?

2. How did the Apostle Paul work with people of other cultures, particularly as a Jew working among Gentiles?

3. What things must we learn about people of other cultures in order to be able to witness effectively to them?

4. What kinds of churches will people of other cultures be most likely to join?

5. How should we train pastors to serve in other cultures?

6. How do we work with a handful of people from another culture when we don't have enough Chris-

tians from that culture to start another church or conduct separate worship services?

7. Do you have other ethnic groups within a twenty-minute drive of your church? What are you doing to reach them? Is any church attempting to reach them? If so, how?

8. How can transfer growth mislead us?

9. How ought one church best go about multiplying itself into other parts of the mosaic? How will such multiplication differ from one part of the country to another, e.g., between urban areas and rural areas?

10. How do educational and financial considerations affect the task of multiplying congregations?

13
The Art of Witnessing to the Atheist/Agnostic

Charles Colson

> Now it is our preference that decides against Christianity, not arguments.
>
> Friedrich Nietzsche

Many conversions are described as foxhole conversions. Maybe so. My own conversion in the midst of Watergate certainly was greeted with skepticism. The cartoonists were busy for months with caricatures of Nixon's tough guy turned to God. But fourteen years later I can write that

I, like Malcolm Muggeridge, am more certain of the existence of God than I am of my own.

I understand, however, how people can listen sympathetically to stories like mine and still doubt. Just because we need God does not prove He exists. This was, of course, Sigmund Freud's central point: that religion perseveres because people need it. "A theological dogma might be refuted [to a person] a thousand times," he wrote. "Provided, however, he had need of it, he again and again accepts it as true."[1]

The influential German philosopher Ludwig Feuerbach believed that God was made in the image of man, a creation of the human mind projecting into the universe. And Karl Marx saw religion as nothing more than an opiate used by the powerful to tranquilize the exploited masses.

If these arguments are correct, then today's battle over the role of religion relates to the need for a psychological prop. If we create God for our individual needs and to civilize culture, then the secularist is right: religion *is* merely a personal illusion and has no place in political affairs.

But if there is strong objective evidence for the existence of God, if He is not a psychological prop but a fact, then we are dealing with the central truth of human existence. And if that is the case—if He exists—then God's role in human affairs, or religion's role in public life, is indeed the most crucial issue of this or any age.

So while it may seem an intrusion, please join me briefly as I relate a few of the evidences of God's existence and character that I have found convincing. For without such evidence, there is no point in your reading this chapter—or my writing it.

It was the very question of God's existence that created the most serious stumbling block to my own conversion.

That August night in 1973 when my friend Tom Phillips first told me about Christ, I told him I wanted no part of foxhole religion. And though later I tearfully called out to God, my mind still rebelled. I needed to know: Was this simply an escape from the trouble I was in? Was I having some sort of emotional breakdown? Or could Christianity be real? I needed evidence.

I started with the copy of *Mere Christianity* Tom had given me. In C. S. Lewis's book I confronted powerful intellectual arguments for the truth of Christianity for the first time in my life.

The existence of God cannot be proved or disproved, of course, but the evidence can be rationally probed and weighed. Lewis does so compellingly, and he cites moral law as a key piece of evidence. Clearly it is not man who has perpetuated the precepts and values that have survived through centuries and across cultures. Indeed, he has done his best to destroy them. The nature of the law restrains man, and thus its very survival presupposes a stronger force behind it: God.

Or consider the most readily observable physical evidence, the nature of the universe. One cannot look at the stars, planets, and galaxies, millions of light-years away, all fixed in perfect harmony, without asking who orders them.

For centuries it was accepted that God was behind the universe because otherwise "the origin and purpose of life [would be] inexplicable."[2] This traditional supposition was unchallenged until the eighteenth century's Age of Reason, when enlightenment thinkers announced with relief that the origins of the universe were now scientifically explainable. What we now call the "big bang theory" rendered the God hypothesis unnecessary.

Although this theory has captured the imagination of many, it leaves serious questions unanswered. Who or what made the big bang? What was there before it? And how in the big bang process—a presumably random explosion—did planet earth achieve such a remarkable, finely developed state? William Paley, the eighteenth-century English clergyman, told what has become a well-known parable on this point. A man walking through a field discovers first a stone, then an ornate gold watch. The stone, the man may reasonably conclude, has simply always been there, a sliver of mineral chipped from the earth by chance. But the watch, which has beauty, design, symmetry, and purpose, did not just happen. It has to have been made by an intelligent, purposeful Creator.

Some have asserted that the universe was self-generated. This violates, however, a primary law of logic: the law of noncontradiction that says the universe cannot be itself *and* the thing it creates at the same time.

Others simply state that the universe itself is self-existent and infinite; it always has been. Yet modern science has discovered no element in the universe that is self-existent. Granted, the whole can be greater than the sum of the parts, but can it be of a different character altogether? Clearly not.

Nonetheless this is the view widely expressed today, most popularly by Carl Sagan, who proposes that "the Cosmos is all that is or ever was or ever will be."[3] That is simply another way of saying that the universe itself is transcendent. Though Sagan's films and books are widely used in schools as science, his argument is, in fact, only theory. It is also no more than an acknowledgment that we do not know how the universe began.

At one point or another even the most obstinate atheist or agnostic must deal with this question of first cause.

During the Watergate scandal, though a new Christian, I approached one of my colleagues to offer spiritual help. "No thanks," he replied. "I'm a rationalist." He tapped his head and said, "It's all in human will. I've thought it all through." He was a confirmed atheist and proud of it.

Since that time I've watched this man not only survive but recover remarkably. He served his prison term without apparent ill effect, wrote memoirs, built a successful business, and kept his family intact. If anything, he appeared stronger for the ordeal.

Then, a few years ago, I learned that he was reading Christian literature. I wrote to him, and he replied that he was indeed seeking. "I'm now an agnostic," he wrote. "I can no longer be an atheist, for I cannot get by the question of the first cause—that is, how life began. The scientific rationales are simply irrational."

Even if modern scientific theories provided satisfactory explanations for the origin of the universe, however, the question of the origin of man would still be unanswered.

The prevailing view of Sagan and others is that a chance collision of atoms created life; subsequent mutations over thousands of years evolved into the extraordinarily complex creature we know as man.

If this is true, man is nothing more than an accident that started as slime or, as one theologian has put it, we are but grown-up germs. Our intuitive moral sense rejects such a trashing of human dignity.

Interestingly enough, even modern scientific research is beginning to question some of its own theories. Given the laws of probability and even allowing for the oldest possible dating of the universe, they ask, has there been enough time for life to begin by random chance and for as utterly complicated a creature as man to evolve?

Weighing the evidence, it is not unfair to suggest that it takes as much faith, if not more, to believe in random chance as it does to believe in a Creator. One can understand why no less a scientist than Albert Einstein, though not of an orthodox faith, felt "rapturous amazement at the harmony of natural law, which reveals an intelligence of such superiority that compared with it all the systematic thinking and acting of human beings is an utterly insignificant reflection." Einstein's belief in the harmony of the universe caused him to conclude, "God does not play dice with the cosmos."[4]

Scientific arguments also fail to take man's basic nature into account: we are imbued with a deep longing for a god. Even an obstinate unbeliever like philosopher Bertrand Russell wrote:

> One is a ghost, floating through the world without any real contact. Even when one feels nearest to other people, something in one seems obstinately to belong to God, and to refuse to enter into any earthly communion—at least that is how I should express it if I thought there was a god. It is odd, isn't it? I care passionately for this world and many things and people in it, and yet . . . what is it all? There *must* be something more important, one feels, though I don't *believe* there is.[5]

When people try to suppress their essential nature, they must either admit the haunting desire for a god, as did Russell, or deal with the inner turmoil through their own means, often with disastrous consequences. Hemingway chose the latter course, as, for that matter, did Marx, Nietzsche, and Freud. Near the end of their lives they were all bitter and lonely men. Nietzsche's insanity, many believe, was due as much to the despair of nihilism as to venereal disease. Freud could not be comforted after his daughter's death, as if he was grieving at the finality of life without God. In his last days Marx was consumed with hatred. All these men were simply reaping the logical consequences of their own philosophies.

But even should we concede that man just happened,

and that he creates his own need for God, how do we explain his need for purpose? Consistent evidence points not only to man's deep spiritual longings but also to a purposeful nature in his desire for community, family, and work.

The great Russian novelist Fyodor Dostoyevski said that not to believe in God was to be condemned to a senseless universe. In *The House of the Dead* he wrote that if one wanted to utterly crush a man, one need only give him work of a completely irrational character, as the writer himself had discovered during his ten years in prison. "If he had to move a heap of earth from one place to another and back again—I believe the convict would hang himself . . . preferring rather to die than endure . . . such humiliation, shame and torture."[6]

Some of Hitler's henchmen at a Nazi concentration camp in Hungary must have read Dostoyevski. There, hundreds of Jewish prisoners survived in disease-infested barracks on little food and gruesome, backbreaking work.

Each day the prisoners were marched to the compound's giant factory, where tons of human waste and garbage were distilled into alcohol to be used as a fuel additive. Even worse than the nauseating odor of stewing sludge was the realization that they were fueling the Nazi war machine.

Then one day Allied aircraft blasted the area and destroyed the hated factory. The next morning several hundred inmates were herded to one end of its charred remains. Expecting orders to begin rebuilding, they were startled when the Nazi officer commanded them to shovel sand into carts and drag it to the other end of the plant.

The next day the process was repeated in reverse; they were ordered to move the huge pile of sand back to the other end of the compound. *A mistake has been made,* they thought. *Stupid swine.* Day after day they hauled the same pile of sand from one end of the camp to the other.

And then Dostoyevski's prediction came true. One old man began crying uncontrollably; the guards hauled him away. Another screamed until he was beaten into silence. Then a young man who had survived three years in the camp darted away from the group. The guards shouted for him to stop as he ran toward the electrified fence. The other prisoners cried out, but it was too late; there was a blinding flash and a terrible sizzling noise as smoke puffed from his smoldering flesh.

In the days that followed, dozens of the prisoners went mad and ran from their work, only to be shot by the guards or electrocuted by the fence. The commandant smugly remarked that there soon would be "no more need to use the crematoria."

The gruesome lesson is plain: Men will cling to life with dogged resolve while working meaningfully, even if that work supports their hated captors. But purposeless labor soon snaps the mind.

You might argue that our need to work was acquired over centuries of evolution. But we must do more than work just to survive; we must do work that has a purpose. Evolution cannot explain this. More plausible is the belief of Jews and Christians that man is a reflection of the nature of a purposeful Creator.

But for those who insist that God is created by man, perhaps the most telling argument is to consider the nature and character of the God revealed in the Bible. If we were making up our own god, would we create one with such harsh demands for justice, righteousness, service, and self-sacrifice as we find in the biblical texts? (As someone has said, Moses didn't come down from the mountain with the Ten Suggestions!)

Would Israel's powerful elite have concocted such declarations as, "He defended the cause of the poor and needy. . . . Is that not what it means to know me?" (Jeremiah 22:16). Would the pious New Testament religious establishment have created a God who condemned them for their own hypocrisy? Would even a zealous disciple have invented a Messiah who called His followers to sell all, give their possessions to the poor, and follow Him to their deaths? The skeptic who believes the Bible's human authors manufactured their God out of psychological need has not read the Scriptures carefully.

"But can we rely on the biblical accounts?" you may ask. When I first became a Christian, I certainly raised such questions. In fact, I began to study the Bible with a lawyer's skepticism. I suspected it was a compilation of ancient fables that had endured through the centuries because of its wisdom.

I made some startling discoveries, however. The original documents from which the Scriptures derive were rigorously examined for authenticity by early canonical councils. They demanded eyewitness accounts or apostolic authorship. Today, a growing body of historical evidence affirms the accuracy of the Scriptures. For example, the prophecy recorded in Psalm 22 explicitly details a crucifixion, with its piercing of the hands and feet, disjointing of the bones, dehydration. Crucifixion, however, was a means of execution unknown to Palestine until the Romans introduced it—several hundred years after the Psalms were written. So modern critics concluded the Psalms were written later, such "prophecies" perhaps even recorded after the fact. Then came the discovery of the Dead Sea Scrolls, which made possible the scientific dating of portions of the Psalms to hundreds of years before Christ.

Modern technology and archeological discoveries are also adding substantial support to the historical authenticity of Scripture. As historian Paul Johnson has written, "A Christian with faith has nothing to fear from the facts."[7]

But sometimes personal experience offers the most convincing evidence. As I have written elsewhere, it was, ironically, the Watergate cover-up that left me convinced that the biblical accounts of the resurrection of Jesus Christ are historically reliable.

In my Watergate experience I saw the inability of men—powerful, highly motivated professionals—to hold together a conspiracy based on a lie. It was less than three weeks from the time that Mr. Nixon knew all the facts to the time that John Dean went to the prosecutors. Once that happened, Mr. Nixon's presidency was doomed. The actual cover-up lasted less than a month. Yet Christ's powerless followers maintained to their grim deaths by execution that they had in fact seen Jesus Christ raised from the dead. There was no conspiracy, no Passover plot. Men and women do not give up their comfort—and certainly not their lives—for what they know to be a lie.

Finally, many of the world's greatest philosophers and scientists have gone beyond deductive assent to the confidence that God exists because they have experienced Him. Were Augustine, Aquinas, Luther, Newton, and the great social reformers of the nineteenth century victims of infantile wish fulfillment? Did some psychological whim motivate St. Francis or George Fox to expend their lives in protest against economic elitism? Was Louis Pasteur, who labored against great physical handicaps to achieve scientific breakthroughs to benefit man, simply mistaken in his motivation to do so for the glory of God?

What is it that motivates people, both Christian and nonbeliever, to do works of mercy? The goodness of the human heart? Hardly. Man's basic nature suggests just the reverse. Rather, love for others, like the need for purpose, is implanted in the hearts and minds of men and women—even those who don't acknowledge it—by a loving and purposeful Creator.

Faith requires no surrender of the intellect. It is not blind, unthinking, and irrational. Nor is it simply a psychological crutch. For me, the objective evidence for God's existence is more convincing than any case I argued as an attorney.

But most rebellion against God is not intellectual. I have met few genuine atheists who would argue passionately that there can be no God. Instead the preponderance of objections are moral and personal. Before his eventual conversion, when philosopher Mortimer Adler was pressed on his reluctance to become a Christian, he replied:

> That's a great gulf between the mind and the heart. I was on the edge of becoming a Christian several times, but didn't do it. I said that if one is born a Christian, one can be lighthearted about living up to Christianity, but if one converts by a clear conscious act of will, one had better be prepared to live a truly Christian life. So you ask yourself, are you prepared to give up all your vices and the weaknesses of the flesh?[8]

It is on the moral level that the most intense battle is being fought for the hearts of modern men and women. If Hemingway and the twentieth-century skeptics are right—if God is dead or irrelevant—then the prospect for true harmony and justice is grim.

Sometimes children understand this profound truth better than adults. Several years ago my son Chris and I were discussing the evidences for God. As I argued that if there were no God, it would be impossible to account for moral law, my grandson Charlie, then four, interrupted.

"But Grandpa," he said, "there is a God." I nodded, assuring him I agreed.

"See, if there wasn't a God, Grandpa," he continued, "people couldn't love each other."

Charlie is right. Only the overarching presence and provision of God assures that both Christian and non-Christian enjoy human dignity and a means to escape our naturally sinful condition. Without His presence, we could not long survive together on this planet.

Discussion Questions

1. Why is it implausible to argue that we created God out of our psychological need?

2. Can the existence of God be proved? Why or why not?

3. How did Watergate help to convince Colson of the reliability of the biblical accounts of the resurrection?

4. Why had Colson's friend shifted from atheism to agnosticism?

5. If we are but "grown-up germs," what right do we have to pronounce something right or wrong or to insist on a standard of rightness?

6. What remarkable admission did Bertrand Russell, the confirmed atheist, make?

7. How does work, particularly the need for purpose in our work, argue for a Creator? What else argues for a Creator?

8. How reliable are the Scriptures and how does that argue for the existence of God?

9. Why does the Bible never argue for the existence of God but always assume the existence of God? *See* Romans 1:19, 20.

10. To what extent is our Christian faith based on facts? What role does human reason play in Christianity?

11. How does it help you to witness to an atheist knowing that most objections to the existence of God are moral and personal?

12. In what sense are both evolutionism and atheism really religions?

13. What do you think of Harry Emerson Fosdick's question to the atheist, "What kind of God don't you believe in? Perhaps I don't believe in that kind of God either"?

Notes

Chapter 2 The Art of Growing in Christ
Mark McCloskey

1. *Sermons and Discourses by Thomas Chalmers* (New York: Robert Carter and Brothers, 1850), pp. 271ff.

2. D. T. Niles, *That They May Have Life* (New York: Harper & Row Publishers, Incorporated, 1951), p. 96.

3. John Greenleaf Whittier, "My Soul and I," in *The Complete Poetical Works of Whittier* (Boston: Houghton Mifflin Company, 1894), p. 428.

4. Leon Morris, *The Gospel According to John* (Grand Rapids, Michigan: William B. Eerdmans Publishing Company, 1971), p. 692.

Chapter 3 The Art of Friendship
Jerry and Mary White

1. Joseph C. Aldrich, *Life-Style Evangelism* (Portland, Oregon: Multnomah Press, 1981), p. 202.

2. Jim Petersen, *Evangelism as a Lifestyle* (Colorado Springs: NavPress, 1980), p. 88.

Chapter 5 The Art of Asking Questions Joel D. Heck

1. Jim Petersen, *Evangelism as a Lifestyle* (Colorado Springs: NavPress, 1980), p. 79.

2. D. James Kennedy, *Evangelism Explosion*, 3d ed. (Wheaton, Illinois: Tyndale House Publishers, 1983), p. 16.

3. Ibid., pp. 24, 25.

4. Stephen J. Biegel, *Speaking of Salvation* (Springfield, Illinois: Stephen J. Biegel, 1977), pp. 26–32.

5. Ada Lum, *How to Begin an Evangelistic Bible Study* (Downers Grove, Illinois: InterVarsity Press, 1971), p. 25.

6. Marilyn Kunz and Catherine Schell, *How to Start a Neighborhood Bible Study*, rev. ed. (Wheaton, Illinois: Tyndale House Publishers, 1981), p. 22.

7. Marilyn Kunz and Catherine Schell, *Mark* (Wheaton, Illinois: Tyndale House Publishers, 1963), p. 16.

8. Martha Reapsome, "People Can Unravel the Bible—if We Let Them," *Evangelical Missions Quarterly*, Vol. 19, No. 3 (July 1983), p. 207.

9. Albert J. Wollen, *Miracles Happen in Group Bible Study* (Glendale, California: Regal Books, 1976), p. 113.

10. Mark Petterson, "Strategic Conversations" in *His Guide to Evangelism* (Downers Grove, Illinois: InterVarsity Press, 1977), p. 45.

11. Rebecca Manley Pippert, *Out of the Saltshaker and Into the World: Evangelism as a Way of Life* (Downers Grove, Illinois: InterVarsity Press, 1979), pp. 138–146.

12. Ibid., p. 138.

13. Erwin J. Kolb, *A Witness Primer* (St. Louis: Concordia Publishing House, 1986), p. 35.

14. Ibid., p. 34.

Chapter 7 The Art of Using Appropriate Vocabulary Dick Innes

1. Peter Cotterell, *Look Who's Talking* (Eastbourne, E. Sussex, England: Kingsway Publications, 1984), p. 14.

2. Ibid., p. 50.

3. Joel D. Heck, "The Vocabulary of Evangelism," *Evangelism*, Vol. 1, No. 2 (February 1987), p. 15.

4. Emory A. Griffin, *The Mind Changers* (Wheaton, Illinois: Tyndale House Publishers, 1976), p. 138.

5. Ibid., p. 137.

6. Cotterell, *Look Who's Talking*, pp. 14, 15.

7. Jim Engel, *Contemporary Christian Communications: Its Theory and Practice* (Nashville: Thomas Nelson Publishers, 1979), p. 26.

8. Dick Innes, *I Hate Witnessing* (Ventura, California: Regal Books, 1983), p. 151.

9. Griffin, *Mind Changers*, p. 142.

10. Gary Smalley and John Trent, *The Language of Love* (Pomona, California: Focus on the Family Publishing, 1988), p. 9.

11. Ibid., p. 10.

12. Rebecca Manley Pippert, *Out of the Saltshaker and Into the World* (Downers Grove, Illinois: InterVarsity Press, 1979), pp. 38, 39.

13. Griffin, *Mind Changers*, pp. 140, 141.

14. Ibid., p. 33.

15. Pippert, *Saltshaker*, pp. 29, 30.

Chapter 8 The Art of Storytelling
Jill Briscoe

1. J. R. R. Tolkien, *The Tolkien Reader* (New York: Ballantine Books, 1966), p. 71.
2. Bruce C. Salmon, *Storytelling in Preaching—a Guide to the Theory and Practice* (Broadman Press, 1988), pp. 10, 11.
3. Ibid., pp. 97, 100.
4. Ibid., p. 22.
5. Ibid., pp. 43, 44.

Chapter 9 The Art of Handling Objections/ Defending the Faith
Charles "Chic" Shaver

1. Charles Colson, *Born Again* (Old Tappan, New Jersey: Chosen Books, Fleming H. Revell Company, 1976), pp. 117–130.
2. James Engel and Wilbert Norton, *What's Gone Wrong With the Harvest?* (Grand Rapids, Michigan: Zondervan Publishing House, 1975), p. 45.
3. Sid is not his real name, but he does represent a real person. Throughout this chapter there will be real-life stories presented, but in each case, I have changed the names to preserve privacy.
4. D. James Kennedy, *Evangelism Explosion*, 3rd ed. (Wheaton, Illinois: Tyndale House Publishers, 1983), p. 77. His whole chapter, "Handling Objections," pp. 77–104, is very helpful.
5. Donald A. Abdon, *Training and Equipping the Saints* (Indianapolis: Parish Leadership Seminars, Incorporated, 1975), pp. 161–174. The quote and the four-step process of handling objections come from the Reverend Abdon's book.
6. Ibid., pp. 161, 162.
7. Paul Little, *How to Give Away Your Faith* (Downers Grove, Illinois: InterVarsity Press, 1966), pp. 67–81.

8. I have amplified Paul Little's answer here by adding from D. James Kennedy, *Evangelism Explosion*, p. 85.
9. This matter of the will and cost of the Gospel are dealt with in an article by Avi Snyder, "The Real Reasons for Disbelief," *Evangelism*, Vol. 3, No. 3 (May 1989), pp. 107–115.

Chapter 11 The Art of Witnessing to the Apathetic
Win Arn and Charles Arn

1. Flavil Yeakley, "A Profile of the New Convert: Change in Life Situation" in *The Pastor's Church Growth Handbook*, Vol. II (Monrovia, California: Church Growth Press, 1982), p. 31.

Chapter 13 The Art of Witnessing to the Atheist/Agnostic
Charles Colson

1. Quoted in R. C. Sproul, *If There Is a God, Why Are There Atheists?* (Minneapolis: Dimension Books, 1978), p. 48.
2. Harry Blamires, *The Christian Mind* (Ann Arbor, Michigan: Servant Books, 1963), p. 44.
3. Carl Sagan, *Cosmos* (New York: Random House, Incorporated, 1980), p. 4.
4. Eugene Mallove, "Gravity: Is the Force That Makes the Apple Fall the Clue to Creation?" in the *Washington Post*, March 3, 1985, p. C-1.
5. Bertrand Russell, *The Autobiography of Bertrand Russell*, a letter to Lady Ottoline Morrell dated August 11, 1918 (Boston: Little, Brown & Company, 1968), p. 121.
6. Quoted in Joseph Frank, *Dostoyevsky: Years of Ordeal* (Princeton, New Jersey: Princeton University Press, 1983), p. 159.
7. Paul Johnson, "A Historian Looks at Jesus," unpublished speech (1986).
8. "Conversation With an Author: Mortimer J. Adler, Author of *How to Think About God*," *Book Digest* magazine (September 1980).

About the Contributors

Ann Kiemel Anderson is a former schoolteacher, youth director, and college dean of women. She divides her time between writing and speaking as well as marathon running and fellowship projects. She and her husband, Will, are the parents of four sons.

Mark McCloskey is the Director of Training and Leadership Development for the U.S. Campus Ministry of Campus Crusade for Christ. He is the author of *Tell It Often, Tell It Well*. McCloskey lives in Minneapolis with his wife and two children.

Jerry and Mary White have been affiliated with The Navigators for many years. Jerry is now General Director and Chief Executive Officer. In addition to ministering to college students and young professional couples, the Whites have written several books separately and together.

Joseph C. Aldrich, President of the Multnomah School of the Bible, is the author of several books, including *Life-Style Evangelism* and *Gentle Persuasion*. He and his wife, Ruthe, are the parents of a son and a daughter.

Joel D. Heck is an Associate Professor of Religion at Concordia University Wisconsin and the editor of *Evangelism* magazine. He and his wife, Cheryl, have three children.

Roy J. Fish, Professor of Evangelism at Southwestern Baptist Theological Seminary, is also a speaker and writer. He and his wife, Jean, are the parents of four children.

Dick Innes, an Australian by birth, is founder and international director of ACTS International, a multichurch service organization that helps churches communicate to the nonchurch community. He is the founding editor of *Encounter* magazine, which is distributed in Australia and New Zealand.

Jill Briscoe is lay director of Women's Ministries at Elmbrook Church in Waukesha, Wisconsin, where her husband, Stuart, is pastor. A popular speaker and writer, British-born Jill is the author of *Queen of Hearts* and *Here Am I, Send Aaron.*

Charles "Chic" Shaver is a Professor of Evangelism at Nazarene Theological Seminary in Kansas City, Missouri. His ministry has included preaching, writing, and the planting and pastoring of two home mission churches.

Moishe Rosen is the Executive Director of Jews for Jesus. Raised as an Orthodox Jew, he came to faith in Y'shua (Jesus) at the age of twenty-one and was later ordained a minister. He is regarded as the leading strategist in the field of Jewish missions. Rosen has written many articles and books, including *Share the New Life With a Jew.*

Win Arn, President of CHURCH GROWTH, INC., is widely recognized as a pioneer of American church growth. He coauthored the best-selling *How to Grow a Church* with the late Donald McGavran.

W. Charles Arn is responsible for research, curriculum development, and communications for CHURCH GROWTH, INC. He edits *Lifeline,* a senior adult church leadership letter, and the Win Arn *Growth Report.*

Donald McGavran, Father of the church growth movement, was a missionary to India for many years. A teacher and writer, he founded the Institute of Church Growth and later became founding dean of the School of World Mission at Fuller Theological Seminary, Pasadena, California. Both Donald McGavran and his wife, Mary, died in 1990.

Charles Colson is Chairman of the Board of Prison Fellowship Ministries. The former special assistant to President Richard Nixon served seven months in prison after pleading guilty to a Watergate-related charge in 1974. His Christian conversion was documented in his first book, *Born Again.*